THIS IS MY BODY

THIS IS MY BODY

By:

H.G. Bishop Raphael

ST SHENOUDA PRESS
SYDNEY, AUSTRALIA
2024

THIS IS MY BODY
The Rite of the Liturgy Explained

COPYRIGHT © 2024
St. Shenouda Press

All rights reserved. Except for brief quotations in critical publications or reviews, no part of this book may be reproduced in any manner without prior written permission from the publisher.

ST SHENOUDA PRESS
8419 Putty Rd,
Putty, NSW, 2330
Sydney, Australia

www.stshenoudapress.com

ISBN 13: 978-0-6457704-5-2

All scripture quotations, unless otherwise indicated, are taken from the New King James Version®. Copyright © 1982 by Thomas Nelson, Inc. Used by permission. All rights reserved.

Cover Design:

Mina Rizkalla
www.minarizkalla.com.au

Cover Imag:

With kind permission from UK Coptic Icons
https://www.ukcopticicons.com/

Contents

Concepts about the Divine Liturgy	7
What is the Liturgy?	17
The Sanctification	23
Offering of the Lamb	27
Thanksgiving Prayer	67
The Covering	75
The Absolution	79
Liturgy of the Word	83
The Litanies	99
Covering Prayer	155
Prayer of Reconciliation	159
Agbeya	181
Repentance	185
Incense	205
Saints in the Liturgy	223

CHAPTER 1

Concepts about the Divine Liturgy

The divine liturgy is considered the most important spiritual act performed by the Church, as it is the essence of spiritual life. One cannot imagine the Church without the liturgy, and Christianity itself cannot be conceived without it. The central doctrine in Christianity is the Incarnation, meaning that God took on a body and became man In the liturgy we unite with this divine body, therefore, explaining the incarnation in the absence of the Eucharist is merely a theoretical and philosophical exercise that lacks practical grounding. Consequently, the story of the Incarnation becomes a historical tale, a narrative told to people, nothing more, and an unexplained belief for non-Christians. Truly… why did God incarnate? And what necessity compelled God to become human? Was there no other way to achieve salvation without the Incarnation? Is God incapable of finding an alternative solution? The sufficient and satisfactory answer is that God incarnated to leave us His sacred body to consume, thereby uniting with Him and obtaining life through Him.

He says to us, "As the living Father sent Me, and I live because of the Father, so he who feeds on Me will live because of Me" (John 6:57). As for how we consume it, Christ himself explained that we are invited to eat it in reality, not just symbolically. We eat His real body in the form of bread and drink His real blood in the form of wine, as He said: "Whoever eats My flesh and drinks My blood has eternal life, and I will raise him up at the last day." (John 6:54). "He who eats My flesh and drinks My blood abides in Me, and I in him." (John 6:56). He undoubtedly meant His actual body present on the altar in the form of bread and wine when He said, " For My flesh is food indeed, and My blood is drink indeed." (John 6:55). The body and blood present on the altar are the culmination and explanation of the divine Incarnation. God in Their Midst

"God is in the midst of her; she shall not be moved" (Psalm 46:5)The liturgy has made the life of the Lord Jesus present every day on the altar. This is what the Lord of glory meant when He said, "Do this in remembrance of me" (1 Corinthians 11:24). In every liturgy, we remember and live the life of Christ in all its details—His passion, death, resurrection, ascension, and His second coming—all present in the liturgy. The phrase "Do this in remembrance of me" means the presence of Christ with us. When we see Him on the altar, we know that His incarnation is not just history but a living reality. The person of the Lord Jesus becomes a daily experience, not a mythical figure. Therefore, one cannot truly imagine Christianity without the liturgy.

One Accord

"These all continued with one accord" (Acts 1:14). Since the beginning, from the time of our apostolic fathers until today, the Church lives through the liturgy.

- Communion is through the liturgy.

- Baptism is not far from the liturgy.

- Prayers for the departed occur during the liturgy.

- Celebrating the feast of a saint is through the liturgy.

- Even the sacrament of unction of the sick (which is allowed to be performed outside the church) is also connected to the liturgy, as the priest takes the "artophorion"[1] after the liturgy to administer to the sick at home or in the hospital.

---

1 Also referred to as pyx or litiya box, or in Arabic (hok al zakheera), is a special and consecrated box the priest takes the Eucharist in to administer to those who are sick or dying.

And the sacrament of marriage is completed in the liturgy, and even now, the bride and groom make sure to partake on the day of their crowning.

Therefore, all our worship and spiritual and church life is connected to the liturgy.

Collective Prayers

The liturgy is one of the collective prayers that we pray together in the church. In addition to the personal prayers that each individual prays alone in their home and room. We are obliged to pray together in collective prayers with one accord.

In the discourse of our Lord Jesus about prayer, He made two points explaining these two types of prayer:

Firstly: "But you, when you pray, go into your room, and when you have shut your door, pray to your Father who is in the secret place; and your Father who sees in secret will reward you openly." (Matthew 6:6). Here, He speaks about personal prayers that an individual prays alone.

Secondly: "And when you pray, do not use vain repetitions as the heathen do, for they think that they will be heard for their many words" (Matthew 6:7). "In this manner, therefore, pray: Our Father in heaven... Give us this day our daily bread. And forgive us our debts, as we forgive our debtors..." (Matthew 6:9-15). Here, all the speech is in the plural form. He did not say, "Pray in this way: My Father who is in heaven... Give me my daily bread... Forgive my sins... As I also forgive." This substantiates the existence of communal prayers that believers pray with one accord using the words known to all. This is what was said about our apostolic fathers concerning their gathering for prayer: "These all continued with one accord in prayer and supplication" (Acts 1:14). The phrase "with one accord" means with one word, one melody, one agreed-upon text (like the hymn book used in spiritual meetings) and one heart. "When the Day of Pentecost had fully come, they were all with one accord in one place" (Acts 2:1).

And when Peter was imprisoned, the whole church gathered to pray "with one accord." So, the phrase "with one accord" expresses the nature of prayer in the church. No one speaks with their own words, but we pray with one accord. The Lord Jesus said: "And whatever you ask in My name, that I will do, that the Father may be glorified in the Son. If you ask anything in My name, I will do it" (John 14:13-14). So, in the liturgy, we have a promise from the Lord Jesus Himself that we obtain what we desire when we stand before Him to pray in His name. He also said: "Again I say to you that if two of you agree on earth concerning anything that they ask, it will be done for them by My Father in heaven" (Matthew 18:19). How much more so, when the whole church agrees through words of prayer and prays them all together with one accord. The nature of prayer in the liturgy is communal prayer.

The Divine Liturgy

The Mass is also called "Liturgy." "Liturgy" is a Greek word consisting of two parts:

The first: "Leitos," meaning "people,"

The second: "Ergon," meaning "work."

The meaning of the word is, therefore, "work of the people," i.e., "a collective work of the people." This Greek word is meant to encompass all the public prayers in the church. And because all public prayers are related to the Mass, the word "Liturgy" has become synonymous with the Mass.

The liturgy fulfills the meaning of the Church as the body of Christ and a congregation of believers. Without uniting with the body of Christ in the Eucharist, the people of God cannot be united together in one entity. The Eucharist is the sacrament of the one Church.

Saint Augustine says: "When we eat ordinary food, we transform it into our bodies. When we eat and drink the sacraments, we are made a part of what we eat and drink, into members in the body of Christ, and it is not we who transform Him into our souls or bodies.

So, the liturgy is essentially the sacrament of gathering the separate individuals into One."

The liturgy sanctifies:

- It sanctifies the offerings.

- It sanctifies the person present for the prayers.

- It sanctifies the place, making it a "holy church."

- It sanctifies everything inside this place (which is the church).

- Even the time in which we pray the liturgy becomes holy.

- Also, the veil, the altar cloths, the cross, the altar, the ambon[2], the books, all become holy through the prayers prayed in the liturgy.

The epitome of sanctification is for the "bread and wine" to turn into the "true body and precious blood of the Lord," and also for the human being to be sanctified. That's why we say in the liturgy: "The holies for the holy." This is the action of the liturgy in us, transforming us into saints qualified to partake in the holies.

Saint Irenaeus says: "Just as earthly bread, by the blessing of God, ceases to be ordinary bread but becomes Eucharistic, composed of earthly and heavenly bread, so also our bodies, after participating in the divine Eucharist, are no longer corrupt but have the hope of resurrection."

During the litanies, we sanctify the world and the entire material creation. We pray for the salvation of the world, the waters, the air, the seeds, the fruits, and the animals. In the liturgy, we perform a sanctifying act for all of life.

The Anaphora

Another name for the liturgy is "Anaphora," which is also a Greek word meaning "to carry up":

---

2 Aka. Analogion or mangaleya. Where the deacon or priest read the liturgical readings

- "Ana": Ascending, Elevated,

- "phero": carrying

In the liturgy, we ascend with the prayers to heaven, provided there is heart and mind readiness. Therefore, the first phrase after the prayer of reconciliation in the liturgy is: "Ano imon tas kardias" (Lift up your hearts). This phrase is kept in Greek in the Coptic translation to preserve the word "Ano" (lift up), from which the word "Anaphora" (carry up) is derived.

Before that, the priest says: "The Lord be with you." The people respond: "And with your spirit." Then: "Ano imon tas kardias" (Lift up your hearts). The people say: "They are with the Lord." Afterward, the priest says: "Efkharisti sumin to Kyrio" (Give thanks to the Lord). This phrase is also kept in Greek because of the word "Efkharistia," which means "the sacrament of thanksgiving." Thus, when the Church coined these phrases, it was expressing the nature of the liturgical prayer. In the liturgy, we declare the Lord's presence with us, lift our hearts to Him, and then thank Him. Therefore, these phrases were placed at the beginning of the liturgy after the prayer of reconciliation and at the beginning of the Anaphora. Thus the priest makes three declarations:

1. "The Lord be with you."

2. "Lift up your hearts."

3. "Give thanks to the Lord."

Other Names for the Liturgy

1. Breaking of the Bread: This is the old biblical expression used by the believers in the apostolic era.

   - "And they continued steadfastly in the apostles' doctrine and fellowship, in the breaking of bread, and in prayers" (Acts 2:42).

   - "Now on the first day of the week, when the disciples came together to break bread, Paul, ready to depart the next day, spoke to them and continued his message until midnight" (Acts 20:7).

- "Then, when he had come up, and had broken bread and eaten, and talked a long while, even till daybreak, he departed" (Acts 20:11).

"And when he had said these things, he took bread and gave thanks to God in the presence of them all" (Acts 27:35).

"So continuing daily with one accord in the temple, and breaking bread from house to house, they ate their food with gladness and simplicity of heart" (Acts 2:46)

This expression was used because the Lord Jesus broke the bread when instituting the sacrament. "And He took bread, gave thanks and broke it, and gave it to them, saying, 'This is My body which is given for you; do this in remembrance of Me'" (Luke 22:19). He did the same thing with the two disciples on the road to Emmaus, so their eyes were opened and knew that it was Him "Now it came to pass, as He sat at the table with them, that He took bread, blessed and broke it, and gave it to them" (Luke 24:30) "And they told about the things that had happened on the road, and how He was known to them in the breaking of bread." (Luke 24:35).

St Paul the Apostles also uses the same expression when writing about the sacrament of the Eucharist "The cup of blessing which we bless, is it not the communion of the blood of Christ? The bread which we break, is it not the communion of the body of Christ?" (1 Corinthians 10:16).

2. Spiritual Sacrifice: Given our Lord Christ offered Himself as a sacrifice on the cross once and the cross is sustained and endures in the sacrifice of the Eucharist. "Therefore, when He came into the world, He said: 'Sacrifice and offering You did not desire, but a body You have prepared for Me'" (Hebrews 10:5).

3. Prosphora: This is a Greek word meaning "offering" because we offer in it our offerings to God, and our tongue states: "From You is everything, and from Your hand, we have given You" (1 Chronicles 29:14).

4- Secrets or Holy Mysteries: Because the action in them is a hidden sacramental action, invisible, but we perceive it by faith. Faith is "the substance of things hoped for, the evidence of things not seen"

(Hebrews 11:1). We believe in the transformation of bread and wine into the true body and blood of the Lord without seeing it. We do not want to see it because seeing is contrary to faith.

5- Synaxis: It is a Greek word meaning "assembly," sometimes called "the Great Synaxis," referring to the Eucharist in contrast to the "Small Synaxis," which includes the raising of incense, praises and the hours of the Agpeya (Horologion)

6- Eucharist: This is the main name for this sacred sacrament, meaning "thanksgiving." We will discuss it in detail later when explaining the prayer of thanksgiving. The prayers used in the divine liturgy have been compiled in a book called "Kholagy," which is a holy book of prayers.

One Mass on One Altar

In the Coptic rite, only one Mass is celebrated on one altar in one day. Saint Ignatius of Antioch, the martyr from the 1st century AD, said, "Be eager to have only one Eucharist. There is one flesh of our Lord Jesus Christ, and one cup for unity with Him, and one altar."

Components and Parts of the Liturgy

In the Acts of the Apostles, it is written: "And they devoted themselves to the apostles' teaching and the fellowship, to the breaking of bread and the prayers" (Acts 2:42). These four elements constitute the liturgy:

1. "The apostles' teaching" is the readings.

2. "The fellowship" is the communal nature of life and joint prayers within the church, also representing the offerings that were eaten after communion.

3. "The breaking of bread" is communion.

4. "The prayers" includes all the liturgy.

When the Lord Jesus consecrated His sacrifice, offering His holy body and blood to His holy disciples, He used these actions: "And He took bread, and when He had given thanks, He broke it and gave it to them, saying, 'This is my body, which is given for you. Do this in remembrance of me'" (Luke 22:19). These actions form the parts of the liturgy:

- "He took bread" corresponds to the Offering of the Lamb.

- "He gave thanks" corresponds to the prayers of thanksgiving and sanctification.

- "He broke it" corresponds to the Fraction.

- "He gave it to them" corresponds to the hymns of distribution.

- "Do this" corresponds to the command to practice the sacrament throughout generations.

These are the same actions used by the Holy Scripture in the story of the appearance of the Lord Jesus to the disciples of Emmaus: "Now it came to pass, as He sat at the table with them, that He took bread, blessed and broke it, and gave it to them." (Luke 24:30).

Why do we fast before communion?

The practice of fasting before communion was established and known since apostolic times. In the story of the selection of Barnabas and Saul for ministry, it is said: "As they ministered to the Lord and fasted, the Holy Spirit said, "Now separate to Me Barnabas and Saul for the work to which I have called them."" (Acts 13:2). This means they were undertaking leitourgia (ministering) while fasting.

Saint Augustine (4th century) explains this point extensively, saying[3] : "this clear that when the disciples first received the body and blood of the Lord, they had not been fasting.

Must we therefore censure the universal Church because the sacrament is everywhere partaken of by persons fasting? Nay, verily,

---
[3] Book I of Replies to Questions of Januarius. Letter 54 Ch.6

for from that time it pleased the Holy Spirit to appoint, for the honour of so great a sacrament, that the body of the Lord should take the precedence of all other food entering the mouth of a Christian; and it is for this reason that the custom referred to is universally observed. For the fact that the Lord instituted the sacrament after other food had been partaken of, does not prove that brethren should come together to partake of that sacrament after having dined or supped, or imitate those whom the apostle reproved and corrected for not distinguishing between the Lord's Supper and an ordinary meal. The Saviour, indeed, in order to commend the depth of that mystery more affectingly to His disciples, was pleased to impress it on their hearts and memories by making its institution His last act before going from them to His Passion. And therefore He did not prescribe the order in which it was to be observed, reserving this to be done by the apostles, through whom He intended to arrange all things pertaining to the Churches. Had He appointed that the sacrament should be always partaken of after other food, I believe that no one would have departed from that practice. But when the apostle, speaking of this sacrament, says, ""Therefore, my brethren, when you come together to eat, wait for one another. But if anyone is hungry, let him eat at home, lest you come together for judgment. And the rest I will set in order when I come" (1 Corinthians 11:33-34). Whence we are given to understand that, since it was too much for him to prescribe completely in an epistle the method observed by the universal Church throughout the world, it was one of the things set in order by him in person, for we find its observance uniform amid all the variety of other customs."

CHAPTER 2

What is the Liturgy?

Our divine liturgy is the most sublime journey to heaven. We go there to witness and enjoy all its glory, joy, and peace, then quickly return to Earth to tell people about the beauty of heaven and the holy life, saying, "Taste and see that the Lord is good" (Psalm 34:8).

The journey begins on the night before the liturgy with the offering of the evening incense. It is as if we are preparing for this sacred journey through prayer, the offering of incense, and presenting suitable hymns to our compassionate God who invited us to unite with Him in the sacrament of the Eucharist.

At midnight, the church stands to praise its heavenly bridegroom, anticipating and eagerly awaiting the speedy arrival of the Lord, "looking for and hastening the coming of the day of God, because of which the heavens will be dissolved, being on fire, and the elements will melt with fervent heat" (2 Peter 3:12) saying, "Amen. Come, Lord Jesus" (Revelation 22:20).

In the early morning, the church raises the morning incense to complete its preparation to receive the true bridegroom in the heavens. Its heart's desire is expressed in the words:

- "As a deer pants for flowing streams, so pants my soul for you, O God" (Psalm 42:1).

- "O God, You are my God; Early will I seek You; My soul thirsts for

You; My flesh longs for You In a dry and thirsty land Where there is no water." (Psalm 63:1).

After the morning incense, the deacons would have prepared the offerings that we will ascend with to present as a thanksgiving sacrifice to our good God. "Give to the Lord the glory due His name;

Bring an offering, and come into His courts." (Psalm 96:8). The offerings we present are the bread and wine, which we offer to God, and by His grace and the descent of the Holy Spirit upon them, they become the Holy Body and Blood of the Lord.

After bringing the offerings before the sanctuary, we recite the Psalms of the Hours (Canonical Hours or Agpeya), as the Psalms sanctify the offerings. "For it is sanctified by the word of God and prayer" (1 Timothy 4:5). Following the Psalms, the priest presents the "lamb" standing at the altar's entrance, facing the congregation. It is as if he represents God who sees us and orchestrates salvation for us through the sacrifice of His only begotten Son.

During the offering of the lamb, the congregation chants the "Kyrie Eleison" ("Lord, have mercy") 41 times, seeking the mercy of God, echoing the tax collector who prayed, saying, "God, be merciful to me, a sinner!" (Luke 18:13).

Then, the priest gives glory to the Holy Trinity as a sign to start the divine liturgy, and both the deacon and the congregation participate (through a specific response) in this Trinitarian praise.

After the thanksgiving prayer, which begins all our liturgical prayers, we seek forgiveness and permission from the Church Fathers in the Absolution of the Servants. Then, we start the liturgy of the Word, known as the "Liturgy of the Catechumens" so that our souls are prepared to unite with Christ our God through the Holy Scripture. This is because the Gospel and all the readings have a sanctifying act and not just a teaching one. At the end of the sacred readings, we hear the joyful voice saying, "You are now clean through the word which I have spoken to you" (John 15:3).

After the readings, the sermon, and the litanies associated with the

Liturgy of the Catechumens, we recite the Creed proclaiming our holy faith. "But you, beloved, building yourselves up on your most holy faith, praying in the Holy Spirit" (Jude 1:20)

We begin our journey to heaven, ascending on the wings of prayer through the Holy Spirit, surrounded by the assembly of angels and saints.

The first stop in our journey is the "Prayer of Reconciliation," where we declare forgiveness and seek forgiveness from one another, acting upon the teachings of our Lord. He said, "Therefore, if you bring your gift to the altar, and there remember that your brother has something against you, leave your gift there before the altar, and go your way. First be reconciled to your brother, and then come and offer your gift" (Matthew 5:23-24). The Prayer of Reconciliation concludes with the holy kiss, "Greet one another with a holy kiss" (1 Corinthians 16:20).

The priest then begins to announce the commencement of the Anaphora (the sacrifice = the liturgy) with three key phrases:

1. "The Lord be with you."

2. "Lift up your hearts."

3. "Let us give thanks to the Lord."

These three phrases express the nature of the sacrament of the Eucharist. They are:

The presence of the Lord and His attendance in His church with His people.

The elevation of believers to heaven.

A sacrifice of thanks to the Lord for His gifts, the creation He made, and for His precious salvation that He granted us through His abundant grace.

The priest begins by describing the heaven we will reach in our holy journey, speaking of the inhabitants of heaven surrounding the divine throne, praising God and saying, "Holy, holy, holy."

We join them in their praise just as they also participate in ours. "And they sang a new song, saying: 'You are worthy to take the scroll, and to open its seals; for You were slain, and have redeemed us to God by Your blood out of every tribe and tongue and people and nation'" (Revelation 5:9). They sing the hymn of victory and salvation that we share with a voice full of glory, chanting, singing, shouting, and proclaiming, "Amen! Blessing and glory and wisdom, thanksgiving and honor and power and might, be to our God forever and ever. Amen!" (Revelation 7:12).

Then the priest explains the "Story of Salvation" from creation and the fall, preparing for the divine incarnation by the prophets.. "in the last days.... was incarnate and became man and taught us the ways of salvation. He granted us the birth from on high through water and Spirit… gave Himself up unto death… He rose from the dead… He ascended into the heavens and sat at Your right hand, O Father… He has appointed a Day for recompense, on which He will judge the living and the dead, and give each one according to his deeds". These sacred prayers summarize for us God's story with humanity from the Book of Genesis to the Book of Revelation.

Then the priest tells us the story of establishing the sacrament by the hands of the Lord Christ: "He took bread in His pure hands… gave thanks, blessed it, sanctified it, broke it, and gave it to His disciples… Take, eat of it, all of you… Do this in remembrance of Me." The same with the cup: "Take, drink of it, all of you, this is My blood." The priest asks, and thus the Holy Spirit descends on the oblation and transforms them into the true body and blood of the Lord.

In the presence of the Lord Christ with us on the altar in His body and blood, we ask of Him our petitions or "litanies".

Then, we remember the assembly of saints present with us in the spirit, believing that during the liturgy, heaven opens on earth, and the heavenly beings share with earthly beings in prayer and praise to God. "Who has established the rising of the choir of the incorporeal (angels and heavenly beings) among men, who has given to the earthly the praising of the seraphim".

And we conclude the "commemoration of the saints" with a commemoration for our fathers and brothers who preceded us and fell asleep in faith in Christ, so that the Lord may repose them in the paradise of joy.

The priest begins to divide the body of Christ, preparing for distribution to the believers. The division of the body symbolizes the salvific sufferings of Christ. Therefore, during the distribution, he chants somewhat sad melodies.

After the fraction, the congregation prays the Lord's Prayer, and the priest prays the absolutions for the forgiveness of sins. Then, with great joy, he announces that the "Holies (the body and blood) are for the holy (for the believers who will now partake)". For we have become saints through the action of the liturgy and the work of the Holy Spirit.

The priest recites the "Holy Confession," stating that what is before him is the true body and blood of our Lord Christ. We approach to partake of them with thanksgiving, humility, reverence, and joy, to receive salvation, forgiveness of sins, and eternal life through them.

During the distribution of the holy mysteries, we chant suitable melodies for this great joy and precious salvation that has come to humanity. When the distribution is complete, the priest dismisses us, saying, "Go in peace." This does not mean just to leave but to proclaim "what great things the Lord has done for you, and how He has had compassion on you." (Mark 5:19)… Just as Christ said to His pure disciples:

"Go, therefore, and make disciples of all nations, baptizing them in the name of the Father and of the Son and of the Holy Spirit" (Matthew 28:19).

"Go into all the world and preach the gospel to every creature" (Mark 16:15).

"Go your way; behold, I send you out as lambs among wolves" (Luke 10:3).

Or as He said to the man healed from demonic possession:

Go home to your friends, and tell them what great things the Lord has done for you, and how He has had compassion on you" (Mark 5:19).

We return from the church to our homes and to the community, or rather from heaven to earth, to witness to Christ who loved us, hoping that we will gather again tomorrow for the same heavenly journey, until the day we dwell there permanently and do not return to earth.

CHAPTER

3

The Sanctification

The Lord Christ is the great High Priest, and during the Great Lent, we chant a hymn in the same vein (Meghalo archi-erevs).

"Seeing then that we have a great High Priest who has passed through the heavens, Jesus the Son of God, let us hold fast our confession." (Hebrews 4:14).

"For such a High Priest was fitting for us, holy, harmless, undefiled, separate from sinners, and has become higher than the heavens" (Hebrews 7:26).

"Now this is the main point of the things we are saying: We have such a High Priest, who is seated at the right hand of the throne of the Majesty in the heavens" (Hebrews 8:1).

Therefore, we believe that the Lord Christ is the worker in the Christian priesthood. He is the one who hears the confession that enters the priest's ears, gives the absolution with His Holy Spirit, baptizes through the hand of the priest, and offers the holy Body and Blood to the believers. He is the one who crowns the bride and groom. In general, He is the one working through His blessed priest.

"For it is God who works in you both to will and to do for His good pleasure" (Philippians 2:13), "I planted, Apollos watered, but God gave the increase" (1 Corinthians 3:6).

The divine liturgy translates this concept into practical action. To understand the depth of this practice, let me mention a liturgical rule in the Coptic Church:

When the priest attends any liturgical prayer, he leads the prayers, and neither the deacon nor any of the worshippers are allowed to lead the prayer in his presence.

When the bishop attends the prayer, he takes the lead in prayer and gives the blessing to the people. He signs the cross over them and says blessed words like "Peace be with you all." The same applies for any words accompanied by a cross sign and blessing of the people. Neither the priest nor the archpriest is allowed to bless in the presence of the bishop, and he (priest) does not hold the cross in his hand. When the Pope attends, he takes care of all these matters, and neither the bishop nor any rank is allowed to do them in the presence of the Pope, and he (bishop) does not hold the cross or staff in his hand.

In the divine liturgy, after the descent of the Holy Spirit upon the offerings and their transformation into the true body and blood of our Lord, not even the Pope or any ranks are allowed to bless the people or sign the cross over the offerings or the incense on the altar or the people. They do not hold the copper staff. This is because the Chief High Priest, our Lord Jesus Christ, is present on the altar with His body and blood, serving as the High Priest above all. He sanctifies His sacrifice.

"As Christ also has loved us and given Himself for us, an offering and a sacrifice to God for a sweet-smelling aroma" (Ephesians 5:2).

"But now, once at the end of the ages, He has appeared to put away sin by the sacrifice of Himself" (Hebrews 9:26).

"For every high priest is appointed to offer both gifts and sacrifices. Therefore, it is necessary that this One also have something to offer" (Hebrews 8:3).

"Not with the blood of goats and calves, but with His own blood He entered the Most Holy Place once for all, having obtained eternal redemption." (Hebrews 9:12).

The sacrifice of the Lord Christ is His holy body, "Therefore, when He came into the world, He said: 'Sacrifice and offering You did not desire, but a body You have prepared for Me'" (Hebrews 10:5).

Returning to the liturgy:

The Holy Spirit descends upon the offerings during the sacrament of the descent of the Holy Spirit. The priest says, "Let Your Holy Spirit descend upon us (pointing with his hands to himself or his head) and upon these gifts set forth (pointing with his hands to the offerings in the paten and the chalice), purify them, change them, and manifest them as a sanctification of Your saints." Then he signs the bread with three quick crosses, saying, "And this bread He makes into His holy Body," and on the cup with three quick crosses, saying, "And this cup also, the precious Blood of His New Covenant".

By saying "body and blood," they become body and blood, so the ritual warns to sign quickly before the transformation because from that moment, no ecclesiastical rank is allowed to sign especially on the body and blood or on the people, as mentioned earlier.

Also, at the end of the liturgy, specifically after the gathering and the dismissal, and at the end of the prayer "Lead us, O Lord, into Your kingdom," when the priest says, "Peace to all," he does not sign the people with the cross, but bows his head towards the priests and deacons only, and moves slightly away from the altar, as if giving the opportunity for the Lord Christ to sign the people with His holy hand.

In the introduction to the Fraction, the priest takes the holy Body in the palm of his left hand, and inserts his right index finger in the chalice, dipping it in the precious Blood. He then lifts his finger slightly and signs the Blood once, then signs the Body with the Blood. Thus, he has signed the Blood with the Blood and the Body with the Blood.

Before confession, the priest takes the "Ispadikon" from the middle of the body with his right hand very carefully, lifts it to the chalice, and signs the holy Blood with the sign of the cross. Thus, he has signed the Blood with the Body. Then he dips the Ispadikon in the Blood, signs the Body with it three times, then returns the Ispadikon to the chalice, and signs the Blood with the Body one last time, placing the Ispadikon upside down on its back inside the cup (because the sacrifice used to be turned on its back before its sacrifice). All of this is done with great care, with the left hand held under the right, which is holding the body, out of caution and respect.

All of these wonderful ritual procedures indicate one thing: that the Lord Christ is the one who sanctifies His sacrifice, and He is the one who completes the liturgy with His glorious presence in His holy Church. Also, this mutual signing between the Body and the Blood declares that "this Body is for this Blood, and this Blood is for this Body," and that His divinity is not separated from His humanity (the blood) or from His body. Therefore, the body is alive and life-giving.

CHAPTER 4

Offering of the Lamb

"As a lamb without blemish" (1 Peter 1:19)

The Divine Liturgy in our Coptic Church begins with the presentation of the Lamb. This part of the ritual involves selecting offerings and placing them on the altar, presenting them before God for sanctification. The bread transforms into the holy Body of the Lord, and the sacramental wine into the precious blood of Christ.

In the Coptic rite, the presented offering is called the Lamb or Lamb of God, which is the same title given to the Lord Jesus. "John saw Jesus coming toward him, and said, 'Behold! The Lamb of God who takes away the sin of the world!'" (John 1:29). We are redeemed "with the precious blood of Christ, as of a lamb without blemish and without spot" (1 Peter 1:19). "Who Himself bore our sins in His own body on the tree, that we, having died to sins, might live for righteousness—by whose stripes you were healed" (1 Peter 2:24).

This fulfills the prophecy: " He was led as a sheep to the slaughter; and as a lamb before its shearer is silent, so He opened not His mouth." (Acts 8:32).

John the Revelator envisioned Him as a lamb: "And I looked, and behold, in the midst of the throne and of the four living creatures, and in the midst of the elders, stood a Lamb as though it had been slain, having seven horns and seven eyes, which are the seven Spirits of God sent out into all the earth" (Revelation 5:6).

Saint Athanasius the Apostolic says, "We must prepare to approach the heavenly Lamb and qualify to touch the heavenly food. Let us wash our hands, purify our bodies, and guard our minds from any evil, so that when we are all pure, we deserve to partake of the Word."

The Sacrificed Lamb

The Church has named the bread sanctified in the Eucharist the "Lamb." The term "Lamb" refers to the Lord as well. "Behold! The Lamb of God who takes away the sin of the world!" (John 1:29). Isaiah the Prophet prophesied about Him: "Like a lamb led to the slaughter, and as a sheep before its shearers is silent, so He opened not His mouth" (Isaiah 53:7). Jeremiah the Prophet also prophesied: "I was like a docile lamb brought to the slaughter" (Jeremiah 11:19).

In multiple places in the Book of Revelation, He is mentioned as the slaughtered Lamb, signifying His role as the true sacrifice for human life:

"Worthy is the Lamb who was slain to receive power and riches and wisdom, and strength and honor and glory and blessing!" (Revelations 5:12)

-" for the Lamb who is in the midst of the throne will shepherd them and lead them to living fountains of waters. And God will wipe away every tear from their eyes." (Revelation 7:17).

- "They overcame him [the dragon] by the blood of the Lamb and by the word of their testimony, and they did not love their lives to the death" (Revelation 12:11).

- "These are the ones who were not defiled with women, for they are virgins. These are the ones who follow the Lamb wherever He goes. These were redeemed from among men, being firstfruits to God and to the Lamb" (Revelation 14:4).

- "These will make war with the Lamb, and the Lamb will overcome them, for He is Lord of lords and King of kings; and those who are with Him are called, chosen, and faithful" (Revelation 17:14).

The Lord Jesus is the incarnate God who accepted to be a sacrificed Lamb for the life of the world. This is the true offering. We, too, must offer ourselves as a sacrifice of love to the God who loved us. "I beseech you, therefore, brethren, by the mercies of God, that you present your bodies a living sacrifice, holy, acceptable to God, which is your reasonable service" (Romans 12:1).

This mutual love is expressed in the Divine Liturgy during the deacon's call in the response: "Greet one another." In the phrase "offer in order". The meaning of "order" is "schematic" or "example" to alert the minds of the people to offer their gifts, hearts, and possessions in the example that was given by our Lord Jesus Christ.

He loved those in the world dearly, loved them to the end, and gave Himself for all of us with joy, love, and delight. He is ready to give to the end. We, too, must offer ourselves in the same way and example.

"We love Him because He first loved us" (1 John 4:19), and "Greater love has no one than this, than to lay down one's life for his friends" (John 15:13). He commanded us with His pure mouth, "A new commandment I give to you, that you love one another; as I have loved you, that you also love one another" (John 13:34).

Lord Jesus, the Beloved, let me present myself at Your feet. My time, effort, wealth, health, and well-being, my sight, hearing, speech, and all that I have—I offer them under Your pure feet in surrender, consecration, love, and joy. I acknowledge that what I have is a pure gift from Your goodness, O Lover of mankind. Our teacher, the Apostle Paul, drew my attention to Your gifts when he said, "What do you have that you did not receive? Now, if you did indeed receive it, why do you boast as if you had not received it?" (1 Corinthians 4:7). Indeed, I do not own myself because You granted me life from nothing. When I fell and was in danger, You reconciled me through Your divine incarnation.

You brought me back into existence and eternity because of Your righteousness and love for humanity. I am Yours for two reasons: first, because you created me, and second, because You bought me with your blood and brought me to life with your power after I died.

"And he died for all, that those who live should no longer live for themselves but for Him who died for them and rose again." (2 Corinthians 5:15).

So, I present myself to you, also 'from what is Yours.'

As for the "offering up of Himself (Christ)",' it was said in the letter to the Hebrews about the Lord Christ: "who does not need daily, as those high priests, to offer up sacrifices, first for His own sins and then for the people's, for this He did once for all when He offered up Himself." (Hebrews 7:27). And, "For every high priest is appointed to offer both gifts and sacrifices. Therefore it is necessary that this One also have something to offer" (Hebrews 8:3).

The thing that the Lord Christ presented for us is His sacred Body on the cross, and we enjoy daily on the holy altar, the same body that was offered on the cross. The liturgy is not a repetition of the cross but its continuation. This holy offering is prophesied in the Psalms: "Give unto the Lord, O you mighty ones, give unto the Lord glory and strength." (Psalm 29:1). And it is prophesied by the prophet Malachi: "For from the rising of the sun, even to its going down, My name shall be great among the Gentiles; in every place incense shall be offered to My name, and a pure offering; for My name shall be great among the nations," Says the Lord of hosts." (Malachi 1:11).

It is noteworthy, in this prophecy spoken by the Holy Spirit through the mouth of the prophet Malachi, that he is talking about the Christian presentation, not the Jewish one. He does not specify a location, rather from the rising of the sun to its setting, and in every place, not just in Jerusalem. He specifies the people as the nations, not just the Jews. He specifies that the offering is 'pure' and there is none pure and holy but God alone, our Lord Jesus.

The Church reminds us that it is not fitting to present only bread and wine to God but a pure heart. "And do not present your members as instruments of unrighteousness to sin, but present yourselves to God as being alive from the dead, and your members as instruments of righteousness to God" (Romans 6:13).

Sacrifice of Thanksgiving

The word 'offering' has both a theological and a spiritual meaning. We offer a sacrifice to God, and God offers a sacrifice on behalf of man, and the two meet in the rite of the liturgy. We offer a sacrifice of thanksgiving, and God bestows a sacrifice of salvation.

Our sacrifice is an expression of gratitude. We take from the fruits of the earth (wheat and wine) and offer them as a sacrifice on the altar, as if we are saying, 'From your hand, we have given you.' We express this in the litany of the oblations by saying, "we offer unto You Your gifts from what is Yours". These are your gifts, Lord, and we offer them to you. Therefore, the Church used the term 'offering", which is a Greek word 'Prosfora,' and from it comes the verb 'Prosferine,' meaning 'present.' The deacon says, "Prosferine, Prosferine", meaning "offer offer", because in the early Church (the first centuries), everyone who came to the Church came with their offering and presented it when the deacon said, 'Prosferine' (offer)… that is offer your gift.. Wheat and wine were placed in the altar, and the rest was stored in the church's store for its needs and the needs of the poor. Everyone who prays in the church must present an offering… a Prosfora.

The Spiritual Sacrifices

These offerings and spiritual sacrifices are what St. Peter referred to in his letter, "you also, as living stones, are being built up a spiritual house, a holy priesthood, to offer up spiritual sacrifices acceptable to God through Jesus Christ" (1 Peter 2:5).

The offering of the lamb in the liturgy is the ideal model for these spiritual sacrifices acceptable to God. Just as the Lord Christ gave Himself for us, presenting Himself as a holy sacrifice to the heavenly Father for the salvation of our race, we should also present a spiritual effort and a sacred toil, an offering of love. "We love Him because

He first loved us." (1 John 4:19). The vigil, fasting, effort in service, the effort spent in studying the Holy Scriptures, caring for orphans, widows, the absent, and the lost—all the effort exerted for the glory of God, the construction of His holy Church, and the salvation of souls—are considered a spiritual sacrifice accepted before God.

Lord Jesus...

When my father the priest offers the lamb before You and to You, my heart lifts up to You, asking that you accept all the offerings of love that we present before You with these oblations. As we bow before you saying, "we are your servants, accept our submission" and cry out in the Gregorian liturgy, "I offer You, O my Master, the symbols of my freedom. I write my works according to Your sayings". If You have given me freedom and freed me from Satan's bonds, then, with my free will and the true desire of my heart, joyfully, I present to You this freedom as an offering of love, to submit to Your tender Fatherhood, to guide my life as You will. Count me as one of Your hired servants.

Perhaps St. Paul the Apostle, in saying, "that I might be a minister of Jesus Christ to the Gentiles, ministering the gospel of God, that the offering of the Gentiles might be acceptable, sanctified by the Holy Spirit." (Romans 15:16), meant by the "offering of the Gentiles", the people who were pagan and whom Paul the Apostle turned to true faith in God. Thus these people became a kind of offering presented to God. This expression was used about the Lord Christ in the Easter Fraction, when He brought the righteous out of Hades and returned them to paradise, "He lifted His saints up on high with Him and gave them as gifts to His Father".

You can present an acceptable offering to God when you turn a sinner away from his deviation or guide a lost soul to the knowledge of divine truth. In this regard, our teacher, the Apostle Paul, said, "Not that I seek the gift, but I seek the fruit that abounds to your account." (Philippians 4:17). This means that what is required is not merely financial contributions; rather, it is better to offer abundant fruits for the glory and edification of the Church—beloved souls for God and lovers of God.

The Offering of Divine Love

The true offering that must be presented is the heart. The offering of the oblations directs the mind to the fact that the heart must be offered to God. We present the "Prosphora" (offering) in the manner of the "Anaphora" (sacred rising offering), and the specific image associated with this offering is "the bread and sacramental wine." The profound spiritual image is "the offering of the life, an offering of love to God."

Offering the Heart with Purity

The priest washes his hands before presenting the offerings, saying during the handwashing, "Purge me with hyssop, and I shall be clean; wash me, and I shall be whiter than snow" (Psalm 51:7), and "I will wash my hands in innocence, so I will go about Your altar, O Lord" (Psalm 26:6). This signifies that the priest cannot present an offering to God unless his heart and internal being are pure. The priest washes his hands with water, not for the mere washing of the hands, but as a reminder that the offering of love ought to be offered with a clean heart and hand.

If the heart is polluted by sin, the offering is rejected before God. The Scriptures state, "The sacrifice of the wicked is an abomination to the Lord" (Proverbs 15:8). How much more when offered deceitfully! The Church's rules prohibits the acceptance of offerings from heretics and evildoers because God does not accept sacrifices tainted with deceit. The "offering of oblations" in the liturgy carries all these beautiful meanings.

White Vestments

Before offering the Eucharistic sacrifice, a prepared heart is offered. The priest washes his hands and, along with the deacons, dons white vestments (tonia) as a symbol of purity. In ancient times, these garments were made of linen, the fabric used to shroud the dead, symbolizing death to the world. The sacrifice cannot be offered to

God unless we are washed, and our hearts are pure and white like the tunic.

The priest prays Psalm 30, "I will extol You, O Lord," and Psalm 92, "The Lord reigns," while putting on the service garments. This is also done by the deacons.

Altar Preparation

Among the preparations is the "altar preparation," setting the heavenly groom's table to be fitting for Christ. Reflecting on the spiritual significance, these preparations point to the heart that offers these sacrifices. God is not concerned with the altar cloths as much as He is with the person offering them.

All the beautiful rituals associated with the presentation of the offering stir the heart to be ready for prayer and communion. During the preparation, the priest prays silently, "O Lord, who knows the hearts of all, who is holy, and who rests in His saints; who alone is without sin and who has power to forgive sins; You, O Lord, know my unworthiness and unpreparedness and my lack of meetness for this Your holy service, and I do not have the countenance to draw near and open my mouth before Your holy glory, but according to the multitude of Your tender mercies, pardon me, a sinner. And grant to me that I may find grace and mercy at this hour, and send down to me strength from on high that I may begin and make ready and accomplish Your holy service after Your pleasure, according to the assent of Your will, for a sweet savour of incense".

Notice that the priest offers repentance and a prepared heart, acknowledging his unworthiness and humbling himself before God. This is so that God may grant him the eligibility and worthiness to serve the liturgy. Before presenting the offering, the priest must present his heart. The congregation, too, offers a repentant and pure heart. Therefore, we chant during the presentation, "Lord, have mercy," forty-one times.

The bread (Korban)

The korban is baked in a special oven called "Bethlehem" or "House of the Offering" as per the Church annex. A specialized person, known as the "custodian" or "offering keeper", oversees the chanting of the psalms during the kneading, pounding, stamping, piercing (making 5 holes) and baking the bread.

The "custodian" or "keeper" is responsible for the church's cleaning, ringing the bell to announce the start of prayer, making the offering, preparing the oil lamps, safeguarding the church doors, caring for church visitors, arranging the church books, church veils, and altar vessels. More than one person may be assigned these tasks, each having specific responsibilities to ensure the church's orderly service. If one is entrusted with cleaning the altar or any internal arrangements, they must hold one of the diaconal ranks.

The best offering and the best heart:

During the presentation, the priest selects the best bread to be the offering for consecration. Likewise, enhance your heart while standing before God. Be eager, prepared, and ready in heart, so that Christ may choose it as an acceptable and pleasing sacrifice. "The sacrifices of God are a broken spirit, a broken and a contrite heart—these, O God, You will not despise" (Psalm 51:17). Therefore, the presentation of the lamb serves as a spiritual lesson for the entire congregation—to be ready and prepared, to be accepted before Christ.

When the priest is choosing the offering lamb, he inspects the bread placed in front of him in the oblation basket so that he chooses the best sacrifice for the eucharist. Why? Because our Lord has been described as, "who committed no sin, nor was deceit found in His mouth" (1 Peter 2:22), which is the fulfillment of the prophecy of the Prophet Isaiah, "because He had done no violence, nor was any deceit in His mouth." (Isaiah 53:9). This was affirmed by the thief on the right who rebuked his companion, saying, "and we indeed justly, for we receive the due reward of our deeds; but this Man has done nothing wrong" (Luke 23:41).

As for the Lord Christ Himself, He said, "Which of you convicts Me of sin?" (John 8:46), and no one dared to open his mouth. For indeed, the Lord Christ was without blame, and despite carrying our sins on His body, He did not sin at all. " For He made Him who knew no sin to be sin for us, that we might become the righteousness of God in Him" (2 Corinthians 5:21). He is truly "in all points tempted as we are, yet without sin" (Hebrews 4:15).

Therefore, the blood of our Lord Christ, our God, is pure and holy Blood that can save all sinners.

"knowing that you were not redeemed with corruptible things, like silver or gold, from your aimless conduct received by tradition from your fathers, but with the precious blood of Christ, as of a lamb without blemish and without spot" (1 Peter 1:18-19).

"how much more shall the blood of Christ, who through the eternal Spirit offered Himself without spot to God, cleanse your conscience from dead works to serve the living God?" (Hebrews 9:14).

"Therefore He is also able to save to the uttermost those who come to God through Him, since He always lives to make intercession for them" (Hebrews 7:25).

If there was any sin or blemish or blame in Him, He would not have been able to save us; instead, it would be said to Him, "Physician, heal Yourself!" (Luke 4:23). Therefore, the Old Covenant sacrifices had the condition that the offered animal should be without blemish. For example, concerning the Passover lamb, it was said, "your lamb shall be without blemish, a male of the first year. You may take it from the sheep or from the goats" (Exodus 12:5). The same was said about the sacrifice of peace:

"And whoever offers a sacrifice of a peace offering to the Lord, to fulfill his vow, or a freewill offering from the cattle or the sheep, it must be perfect to be accepted; there shall be no defect in it. Those that are blind or broken or maimed, or have an ulcer or eczema or scabs, you shall not offer to the Lord, nor make an offering by fire of them on the altar to the Lord. Either a bull or a lamb that has any limb too long or too short you may offer as a freewill offering, but for a vow it shall not be accepted 'You shall not offer to the Lord what is bruised or crushed, or torn or cut; nor shall you make any offering of them in your land." (Leviticus 22:21-24)

These same conditions exist for all the sacrifices. The Prophet Malachi rebuked those who took this matter lightly: " But cursed be the deceiver who has in his flock a male, and takes a vow, but sacrifices to the Lord what is blemished— For I am a great King," says the Lord of hosts, "And My name is to be feared among the nations." (Malachi 1:14).

All of this is because these sacrifices were a symbol of the complete sacrifice of the Lord Christ, which is without blemish or blame. Therefore, the priest also chooses an offering without blemish to be the offering of Christ.

Here is a beautiful note, worthy of contemplation:

In the trial of the Lord Christ, the priests gathered with their leaders to examine Christ, as if they were examining the sacrifice before deciding to sacrifice it. If any fault or blemish was found, it would be rejected; otherwise, it would be offered as a sacrifice. Two sacrifices were presented to the priestly court: (The first: Jesus of Nazareth. The second: Barabbas the murderer). Unlike the civil court, the priesthood court ruled differently. They declared the righteous Jesus to be a suitable sacrifice and released Barabbas sinner.

"And they all cried out at once, saying, "Away with this Man, and release to us Barabbas" (Luke 23:18).

"Crucify Him, crucify Him!" (Luke 23:21).

"His blood be on us and on our children" (Matthew 27:25).

This outcry was incited by the priests, who were unaware of what they were doing, "now this he did not say on his own authority; but being high priest that year he prophesied that Jesus would die for the nation" (John 11:51). Pilate, the Roman governor, wanted to release Jesus because He was innocent, and he found no fault in Him, as confirmed by Herod as well. However, the chief priests had a different judgment. In their view, Jesus was fit to be sacrificed because He was blameless, while Barabbas was not suitable.

When we also realize that the name "Barabbas" means "Son of the Father," we are put in front two sons of the Father, one a true and blameless Son and the other a false and faulty one. Thus, it was just and priestly righteousness to crucify Jesus as a sacrifice for the people, and to release Barabbas because he was of no benefit. Thus, when the priest chooses the offering, he leaves the blemished one and chooses the good one.

Oh Lord Jesus,

I marvel that You choose me for Your divine service, even though I am flawed and filled with defects and shortcomings. But my marvel ceases when I hear your great apostle Paul saying, "but God has chosen the foolish things of the world to put to shame the wise, and God has chosen the weak things of the world to put to shame the things which are mighty; and the base things of the world and the things which are despised God has chosen, and the things which are not, to bring to nothing the things that are, that no flesh should glory in His presence" (1 Corinthians 1:27-29).

Truly you O God are "chief among ten thousand." (Song of songs 5:10)

"For who in the heavens can be compared to the Lord? Who among the sons of the mighty can be likened to the Lord?" (Psalm 89:6).

Specifications of the Chosen Offering:

The chosen offering must be freshly baked on the same day, round, without cracks or deformities. It must be fully leavened, stamped clearly, with the five piercings in their places and the Espadikon intact. The round shape of the offering symbolises eternity because the circle has neither beginning nor end. Similarly, our Holy Christ is eternal, without beginning or end.

Number of loaves in the oblation basket

As for the number of loaves offered, it represents Christ among His holy disciples, whom He "sent out two by two" (Mark 6:7), and their number was 12 or 70. Thus, the offering in the basket represents the apostles with the Lord Christ in their midst, "chief among ten thousand" (Song of songs 5:10), or it represents the believers (even numbers symbolize love and companionship) with Christ among them, distinguished. The father priest seeks this distinguished offering to place it on the altar, and through prayer, it becomes the real body of Christ. Therefore, the number of offerings presented is always an odd number.

Now the question: Why are sometimes 3 offerings presented and other times 5, 7, or more or fewer?

If we consider that the remaining offering will be distributed to the people in the form of the "bread of blessing" (i.e., the antidoron or ologia) after the end of the liturgy, the number of offerings will be proportional to the expected number of people attending the prayer. If a large number of people are expected to attend, many offerings will be offered and one chosen as the sacrificial lamb, and the rest will be left for distribution to the people.

In this matter, there is a contemplation worth stopping at. The attendance of the people to the church in large numbers signifies noticeable active and distinguished service of the church servants and its priests. These servants are deserving of honour and sanctification and can be likened to the oblation bread that is placed next to Christ's oblation bread. Every servant among us that toils in bringing the people to the church to receive salvation through Christ in the sacrament of communion, will receive the honour of being represented by an offering placed beside Christ. However, our Lord Jesus remains the most distinguished (the best offering) because He is God manifest in the flesh, and He is "chief among ten thousand." (Song of songs 5:10). He alone has a pure humanity without blemish or stain. "but with the precious blood of Christ, as of a lamb without blemish and without spot" (1 Peter 1:19).

Also, consider, my friend, the servant that the priest (the servant of the sacrament) will stand at the end of the liturgy to cut these offerings and distribute them as a blessing to the people. This means that you are invited to be torn and broken to be consumed so that the people of Christ may receive the blessing. "For we must labor so that the people may rest."

Signing the bread with the wine

After choosing the best offering to be the body of Christ, the priest signs all the offerings with the wine carried in a vessel by the deacon on his right side. The signing is first for the chosen offering, then for the rest of the offerings, and it concludes with the chosen offering because our Lord Jesus Christ is the beginning and the end. "I am the Alpha and the Omega, the Beginning and the End," says the Lord, "who is and who was and who is to come, the Almighty" (Revelation 1:8).

When the priest signs the offering, he says about the chosen offering at the beginning: "A sacrifice of glory," and at the end: "A royal sacrifice of righteousness". As for the rest of the offerings, he says about them: "A sacrifice of blessing, a sacrifice of honour, a sacrifice of Abraham, Isaac, Jacob, Aaron, Zechariah, Simeon... and so on."

This signing with wine expresses the sanctification of the offering with the substance of the sacrament, which is intended to transform into the blood of Christ, indicating that the Lord Christ sanctifies His sacrifice by Himself. This matter will be repeated during the liturgy several times, and which we will discuss later on.

The fruit of the vine:

Why did the Lord Christ specifically choose the fruit of the vine to be transformed into His holy Blood, and why did He not choose any other fruit product?

The resemblance of Christ and the church to the grapevine is accurately described and beautifully repeated throughout the Holy

Scriptures. Christ is the true vine, "I am the true vine, and My Father is the vinedresser" (John 15:1), and we are the branches (John 15:5). He also said to them in glory, "Abide in Me, and I in you. As the branch cannot bear fruit of itself, unless it abides in the vine, neither can you, unless you abide in Me" (John 15:4).

Every local church is a bunch of grapes in this vine, and the believing members are the grapes. The universal church is the huge vine that includes all these bunches (these creatures in all the earth to the ends of the world).

Christ is the root and origin of this vine. The resemblance of the church to the vine is deeply rooted in all the books of the Holy Bible in both testaments. In the Psalms, "You have brought a vine out of Egypt; You have cast out the nations, and planted it" (Psalm 80:8). Vine here means, the people of God, whom the Lord brought out of the land of Egypt. In the book of Deuteronomy, the prophet Moses speaks of the blessing that God will give to His people, saying, "With the choicest wheat; and you drank wine, the blood of the grapes." (Deuteronomy 32:14). It is not hidden from the discerning reader that "choicest wheat" is the holy Body taken in the form of bread, and the blood of the grape is a very clear indication of the blood of Christ taken in the form of wine. Note here that it did not say grape juice but the blood of the grape to make the reference more explicit.

In the blessing of Isaac, the father of fathers, to his son Jacob, he said, "with grain and wine I have sustained him" (Genesis 27:37). By wheat and wine, he meant that Christ comes from the lineage of Jacob. So when Esau came to take the blessing, "he cried with an exceedingly great and bitter cry, and said to his father, "Bless me—me also, O my father!"" (Genesis 27:34). Then he said to his father, "have you only one blessing, my father? Bless me—me also, O my father!" (Genesis 27:38). His father did not give him wheat and wine like his brother, but said to him, "with grain and wine I have sustained him. What shall I do now for you, my son?" (Genesis 27:37). This indicates that wheat and wine were not meant to be taken literally but symbolically, representing the Body and Blood of the Lord Christ who was born of the lineage of Jacob, not Esau.

The Holy Scriptures repeatedly mention the phrase "blood of grapes" with clear indications that the juice of the vine will transform into the Blood of Christ:

- "The scepter shall not depart from Judah, nor the ruler's staff from between his feet, until tribute comes to him; and to him shall be the obedience of the peoples. Binding his foal to the vine and his donkey's colt to the choice vine, he has washed his garments in wine and his vesture in the blood of grapes" (Genesis 49:10-11).

"curds from the cattle, and milk of the flock, with fat of lambs; and rams of the breed of Bashan, and goats, with the choicest wheat; and you drank wine, the blood of the grapes" (Deuteronomy 32:14).

"The basic necessities of human life are water and fire and iron and salt and wheat flour and milk and honey, the blood of the grape and oil and clothing" (Sirach 39:31).

Therefore, the juice of the vine will transform into the sacred Blood of the Lord. The Church is the vine, as expressed in the hymn: "Lord God of the powers, return and behold from heaven, and look and visit this vine, restore and establish her, this which Your right hand has planted" (Annual Aspasmos Watos). The verse in Psalms also declares, "Return, we beseech You, O God of hosts; look down from heaven and see, and visit this vine" (Psalm 80:14).

Christ is the head of the Church, as stated:

- "And He put all things under His feet, and gave Him to be head over all things to the church" (Ephesians 1:22).

- "But, speaking the truth in love, may grow up in all things into Him who is the head—Christ" (Ephesians 4:15).

- "For the husband is the head of the wife even as Christ is the head of the church, his body, and is himself its Savior" (Ephesians 5:23).

- "And He is the head of the body, the church, who is the beginning, the firstborn from the dead, that in all things He may have the preeminence" (Colossians 1:18).

He is also the root and origin of the vine:

- "There shall be a root of Jesse; And He who shall rise to reign over the Gentiles, In Him the Gentiles shall hope." (Romans 15:12).

- "The Lion of the tribe of Judah, the Root of David" (Revelation 5:5).

- "I am the root and the descendant of David, the bright morning star" (Revelation 22:16).

Thus, when the Church is described as a body, Christ is its head, and we are the members. When described as a vine, Christ is its root, and we are the branches.

Truly it was said regarding the Church and Christ, "Your wife shall be like a fruitful vine in the very heart of your house, your children like olive plants all around your table." (Psalm 128:3). The Church declares, "like the vine, I have born the fruit of a sweet fragrance. And my flowers are the fruit of honour and integrity" (Sirach 24:23). This is the vine for which the Prophet Isaiah sang: "In that day sing to her, "A vineyard of red wine! I, the Lord, keep it, I water it every moment; lest any hurt it, I keep it night and day." (Isaiah 27:2-3). It is the Church of God that He has planted, "It was planted in good soil by many waters, to bring forth branches, bear fruit, and become a majestic vine" (Ezekiel 17:8).

Lord Jesus, let me abide in You, the true vine.

"Abide in Me, and I in you. As the branch cannot bear fruit of itself, unless it abides in the vine, neither can you, unless you abide in Me. I am the vine, you are the branches. He who abides in Me, and I in him, bears much fruit; for without Me you can do nothing" (John 15:4-5).

Wheat

Just as the vine symbolizes the Church and its unity with the Lord Jesus Christ, wheat also symbolizes the Church. Jesus Himself compared Himself to wheat when He said, "Most assuredly, I say to you, unless a grain of wheat falls into the ground and dies, it remains alone; but if it dies, it produces much grain" (John 12:24). He spoke of His death and burial, and the abundant crop refers to believers in His holy name. Certainly, when wheat is sown, it yields wheat.

Therefore, we are conformed to the image of Christ when we are born again through Holy Baptism.

"Ssince you have put off the old man with his deeds, and have put on the new man who is renewed in knowledge according to the image of Him who created him" (Colossians 3:9-10). "For whom He foreknew, He also predestined to be conformed to the image of His Son, that He might be the firstborn among many brethren" (Romans 8:29).

This image, we take its pledge in baptism and it is completed in us through spiritual struggle, so we transform into it gradually (from glory to glory). "But we all, with unveiled face, beholding as in a mirror the glory of the Lord, are being transformed into the same image from glory to glory, just as by the Spirit of the Lord" (2 Corinthians 3:18). It is finally and truly completed in the resurrection, in the eternal bliss, "And as we have borne the image of the man of dust, we shall also bear the image of the heavenly Man" (1 Corinthians 15:49), and "who will transform our lowly body that it may be conformed to His glorious body, according to the working by which He is able even to subdue all things to Himself" (Philippians 3:21).

Returning to our subject... Since Christ is the grain of wheat that died and was buried, bringing forth abundant fruits, we become grains of this wheat resulting from the planting of Christ... These grains are gathered together and ground to become the bread of God in the sacrament of the Eucharist. Jesus Himself mentioned this analogy in the parable of the weeds and the wheat, " but while men slept, his enemy came and sowed tares among the wheat and went his way" (Matthew 13:25). And He explained the meaning of this when he said, "The field is the world, the good seeds are the sons of the kingdom, but the tares are the sons of the wicked one" (Matthew 13:38).

So, John the Baptist said about the Lord Jesus, "His winnowing fan is in His hand, and He will thoroughly clean out His threshing floor, and gather His wheat into the barn; but He will burn up the chaff with unquenchable fire" (Matthew 3:12).

We are God's wheat:

St. Ignatius the God-bearer said when facing the fangs of wild beasts, "I am God's wheat, and I shall be ground by the teeth of wild beasts to become pure bread for Christ."

Therefore, the blessings that God bestowed upon His people on many occasions contain both wheat (the body of Christ) and wine (His precious blood):

- The blessing of Isaac to Jacob: "Therefore may God give you of the dew of heaven, of the fatness of the earth, and plenty of grain and wine" (Genesis 27:28).

- "Then Israel shall dwell in safety, the fountain of Jacob alone, in a land of grain and new wine; His heavens shall also drop dew" (Deuteronomy 33:28).

"Curds from the cattle, and milk of the flock, with fat of lambs; and rams of the breed of Bashan, and goats, with the choicest wheat; and you drank wine, the blood of the grapes" (Deuteronomy 32:14)

"He would have fed them also with the finest of wheat; and with honey from the rock I would have satisfied you" (Psalm 81:16)

"He makes peace in your borders, and fills you with the finest wheat" (Psalm 147:14).

"until I come and take you away to a land like your own land, a land of grain and new wine, a land of bread and vineyards" (Isaiah 36:17).

"The threshing floors shall be full of wheat, and the vats shall overflow with new wine and oil" (Joel 2:24).

"Therefore they shall come and sing in the height of Zion, streaming to the goodness of the Lord—for wheat and new wine and oil, for the young of the flock and the herd; their souls shall be like a well-watered garden, and they shall sorrow no more at all" (Jeremiah 31:12).

"For how great is its goodness and how great its beauty! Grain shall make the young men thrive, and new wine the young women." (Zechariah 9:17).

"The Lord will answer and say to His people, "Behold, I will send you grain and new wine and oil, and you will be satisfied by them; I will no longer make you a reproach among the nations" (Joel 2:19).

The blessing with which Joseph the righteous blessed the world was the stored wheat. He saved the world from the famine, as a symbol of the Lord Christ who saved the world by the bread of His body. Therefore, Pharaoh called Joseph "Zaphnath-Paaneah" (Savior of the world) (Genesis 41:45).

So, in the sacrament of communion, there is a beautiful and wonderful meaning: (The grains of wheat are gathered together in one korbana, and the individual grapes are gathered together in one cup, symbolizing the nature of the united Church of many individuals who have become one in and through Christ. This offering and this cup, through prayer, become the real body and blood of Christ, which we partake of to strengthen and grow in our unity in Christ).

The Korbana as a Symbol of the Church

The offering presented is a model of the Church, consisting of a large group of wheat grains, with each grain representing a Christian. Then the wheat is ground, and this grinding process symbolizes the pain we go through in spiritual life—the pain in asceticism, the fatigue of standing in prayer before God, and also the pains and troubles of service, hardship and persecution. "Blessed are you when they revile… you" (Matthew 5:11).

Therefore, we notice that the strongest churches are those that endured pain and persecution. This is not strange because if the head of the Church, our God, is crucified, then the body (the Church) must also be crucified. If the Church gives up carrying the cross, it will not be the Church of Christ, for the cross is inseparable from the Church.

So, the grains of wheat must be ground and become fine flour. "If anyone would come after Me, let him deny himself and take up his cross daily and follow me" (Luke 9:23), "and he who does not take his cross and follow after Me is not worthy of Me." (Matthew 10:38). Without grinding, each grain remains individual and not united with the others. However, with grinding, it becomes difficult to distinguish between them. The Church transforms from individual scattered members into one body. But the flour has not yet become one body (entity), and how easy it is for it to scatter again. Therefore, water, symbolizing the Holy Spirit, binds the flour into one body, just as the one Spirit makes the Church one by descending upon it. Here, the distinction between the wheat grains cannot be made, and the dough cannot turn back into flour or wheat.

That is, the Church cannot be dissolved; no wheat grain that enters the mill returns to its original nature. The nature of the Church begins and does not end; it goes from isolation to unity, and this becomes the nature of the Church, the body of Christ. The isolated one has not yet shared with us in pain, asceticism, service, and ecclesiastical life, and therefore he remains an individual.

When the offering is placed on the altar, it is as if the Church presents itself as a sacrificial offering of love to her heavenly bridegroom. And when the offering, through prayer and the descent of the Holy Spirit, turns into the real Body of the Lord Christ, it is declared to us that the Lord Christ is the One who presented Himself as a sacrifice for the Church, His pure bride.

It is an epic of love. For Christ, on top of the altar, is sacrificed for the Church, and the Church, under the altar, is sacrificed for Christ.

And I say here that it is below the altar because our teacher John the Seer saw this in the Book of Revelation, "When He opened the fifth seal, I saw under the altar the souls of those who had been slain for the word of God and for the testimony which they held" (Revelation

6:9).

In the middle of the offering, there is a large cross called the "Espadikon" (the master part). It is as if the offering explains to us that the Lord Christ is present in the midst of the Church, gathering around Him the believers who are members of His body. Around the Espadikon, there are twelve small crosses representing the apostles, their successors, and the priesthood in general. The rest of the offering represents the rest of the people of God gathered around it and connected to it through this sacred priesthood. Truly, the Church proclaims: "Emmanuel our God is now in our midst", "Behold, Emmanuel our God… is with us today on this table" (The fraction of the Heavenly).

The presence of the Lord Christ in the midst of the Church is the mystery of its unity and assembly. This presence is clearly proclaimed during the sacrament of the Eucharist. Perhaps the secret of the Church's endurance, vitality, unity, and strength throughout time is its adherence to the sacrament of the Eucharist as a spiritual foundation for all our relationships with God.

The offering on the altar is the magnet that gathers and unifies the entire Church. "For we, though many, are one bread and one body; for we all partake of that one bread" (1 Corinthians 10:17). "Make us all worthy, our Master, to partake of your holies for the purification of our souls, bodies, and spirits, so that we may become one body and one spirit, and find a share and inheritance with all the saints…" (Introduction to the litanies- Basilian Liturgy).

The inscription on the offering also explain the nature of this body. Christ in the midst, surrounded by the priests (the twelve crosses), gathered around Him are the people (the rest of the offering), and written around this pattern in Coptic: "Holy God, Holy Mighty, Holy Immortal". This is the hymn we sing to our powerful and living God who was crucified for us and rose from the dead by the power of His divinity. This hymn is inscribed like a belt around the offering to teach us that the Church is holy because of God's presence in it, the "Most Holy" (Daniel 9:24); as we say in the Divine Liturgy (sanctified us by Your Holy Spirit). Moreover, it is also a confession of the divinity of our Lord Jesus Christ and His power and eternity.

The likening of the Church to the offering is an ancient teaching. Saint Cyprian the Martyr (from the third century AD) says: "For when the Lord calls bread, which is combined by the union of many grains, His body, He indicates our people whom He bore as being united; and when He calls the wine, which is pressed from many grapes and clusters and collected together, His blood, He also signifies our flock linked together by the mingling of a united multitude".

It is also mentioned in the Didache (Teaching of the Apostles), a document from the first century AD: "As this broken bread was scattered on the mountains and then gathered, so let your church be gathered from the ends of the earth into Your kingdom."

The Five Holes in the Offering:

There are five holes around the Espadikon representing the five wounds of Christ (His hands, feet, and side). They are arranged: three on the right of the priest and two on his left as he holds the offering. These precious wounds, were foretold by the Prophet Isaiah, "But He was wounded for our transgressions, He was bruised for our iniquities; the chastisement for our peace was upon Him, and by His stripes, we are healed" (Isaiah 53:5). Our teacher, the Apostle Peter, also said about them, "By whose stripes you were healed" (1 Peter 2:24).

Truly, they are the healing and saving wounds that the Lord Christ spoke about in prophecy, "And one will say to him, 'What are these wounds between your arms?' Then he will answer, 'Those with which I was wounded in the house of my friends.'"(Zechariah 13:6). They are presented before us at all times to remind us of His love and His salvific pains for us. They are the wounds that the bride saw causing her heart to yearn, "My beloved put his hand by the latch of the door, and my heart yearned for him" (Song of Solomon 5:4).

The Yeast:

After that, the dough is mixed with yeast, symbolizing evil. In the

Old Testament, they celebrated the Feast of Unleavened Bread, which is bread without yeast because it symbolizes evil. Our teacher, the Apostle Paul, explained the matter of unleavened bread, saying,"Therefore let us keep the feast, not with old leaven, nor with the leaven of malice and wickedness, but with the unleavened bread of sincerity and truth" (1 Corinthians 5:8).

Why then is yeast, a symbol of evil, placed in the offering?! It is placed to express our sins that the Lord Christ carried in His body for us. "Behold! The Lamb of God who takes away the sin of the world" (John 1:29). The sin of the world was placed on the Lamb so He may lift it from us. Christ alone is sinless, yet He carried all the sins of the world, "For He made Him who knew no sin to be sin for us, that we might become the righteousness of God in Him" (2 Corinthians 5:21).

Afterward, the offering is placed in the fire, and as a result, the yeast withers and dies. Christ carried our sins in His body and ascended with them to the cross to kill sin in the cross' redemptive fire. The offering indeed contains yeast, but it is dead yeast. Similarly, the Church has sin, but it is dead sin. The members of the Church (we the believers) do sin, as no one can claim that we, while on Earth, to be free from error. "If we say that we have no sin, we deceive ourselves, and the truth is not in us" (1 John 1:8). However, the effect of sin is nullified every day through repentance and confession.

Salt is not added to the offering because, as Christ said, "You are the salt of the earth, but if the salt loses its flavor, how shall it be seasoned? It is then good for nothing but to be thrown out and trampled underfoot by men" (Matthew 5:13). Christ's body is the salt that seasons the world and preserves it from corruption, giving it an acceptable taste, therefore, it does not need the addition of salt.

The Church and the Body of Christ:

We speak of the offering as a model to explain the formation and nature of the Church and its connection to Christ in the unity of love. This is before the offering itself transforms through prayer, consecration, and the coming of the Holy Spirit into the real body of the Lord Jesus. In saying this, we must not confuse the meaning between the personal body of Christ born of the Virgin Mary without sin, which we eat on the altar, and the body of Christ, which is the Church, consisting of us as members of this body. "Now you are the body of Christ, and members individually" (1 Corinthians 12:27).

Distinction between the personal Body of Christ and the Church the Body of Christ:

1. The Church was not born of the Virgin Mary; rather, Christ alone is the head of the Church, "and gave Him to be head over all things to the Church" (Ephesians 1:22).

2. The Church was not crucified with Christ; He died alone for us. "I have trodden the winepress alone, and from the peoples no one was with Me" (Isaiah 63:3).

Therefore, Christ said to the Church (the assembly of the apostles), "Behold, the hour is coming, and has now come, that you will be scattered, each to his own, and will leave Me alone. And yet, I am not alone because the Father is with Me" (John 16:32).

3. Christ is our redeemer because He was crucified alone for us. If the Church were crucified with Him, how could He be a redeemer for us?

He is a redeemer because He died in place of us and on our behalf. We did not die with Him on the cross because we were not present then. We received our share in His cross when we were baptized in His holy name.

"Therefore we were buried with Him through baptism into death, that just as Christ was raised from the dead by the glory of the Father, even so we also should walk in newness of life. For if we have been united together in the likeness of His death, certainly we also shall be in the likeness of His resurrection" (Romans 6:5).

"Buried with Him in baptism, in which you also were raised with Him through faith in the working of God, who raised Him from the dead. And you, being dead in your trespasses and the uncircumcision of your flesh, He has made alive together with Him, having forgiven you all trespasses" (Colossians 2:12-13).

Therefore, only after baptism can we rightly say:

"I have been crucified with Christ; it is no longer I who live, but Christ lives in me; and the life which I now live in the flesh I live by faith in the Son of God, who loved me and gave Himself for me" (Galatians 2:20)

"Knowing this: that our old man was crucified with Him, that the body of sin might be done away with, that we should no longer be slaves of sin" (Romans 6:6).

As for the cross itself, the Lord Christ was crucified alone because He "loved me and gave Himself for me" (Galatians 2:20). If the Church were the body of Christ crucified, its members would not need to be baptized. However, the opposite is true. We need baptism to be crucified with Him, buried with Him, and rise again, "and raised us up together, and made us sit together in the heavenly places in Christ Jesus" (Ephesians 2:6).

4- The Church also shares in the pains of the cross, enduring all kinds of suffering for the sake of Christ. "And whoever does not take his cross and follow me is not worthy of me" (Matthew 10:38). It is the cross of the pains of persecution, the pains of service and its toils, the pains of asceticism and its hardships, and the natural pains. "Knowing that the same kinds of suffering are being experienced by your brotherhood in the world" (1 Peter 5:9). Yet, we endure them with gratitude, becoming partners in the cross of Christ.

- "This is a faithful saying: For if we died with Him, We shall also live with Him. If we endure, We shall also reign with Him. If we deny Him, He also will deny us" (2 Timothy 2:11-12).

- "If indeed we suffer with Him, that we may also be glorified together" (Romans 8:17).

As for the crucifixion on Golgotha, there was no one there but Jesus Christ alone with His own body which is given the life of the world.

5- The crucified body of Christ for us is a body without blemish, blame, or sin.

- "How much more shall the blood of Christ, who through the eternal Spirit offered Himself without spot to God, cleanse your conscience from dead works to serve the living God?" (Hebrews 9:14).

- "With the precious blood of Christ, as of a lamb without blemish and without spot" (1 Peter 1:19).

As for us, the members of the Church, "If we say we have no sin, we deceive ourselves, and the truth is not in us... If we say we have not sinned, we make Him a liar, and His word is not in us" (1 John 1:8, 10). But Christ "poured out His soul unto death, And He was numbered with the transgressors" (Isaiah 53:12). Thus, it was said of Him: "For our sake, He made Him to be sin who knew no sin so that in Him we might become the righteousness of God" (2 Corinthians 5:21). He bore the sins of the Church on His own body so that we may become righteous in Him.

6- The body of Christ, born of the Virgin and unique to Him, is united hypostatically with His divinity, like the union of the soul with the body in man. Christ, on the other hand, united with His Church, is like the union of a man with his wife. Thus, the Church becomes His body, just as the woman is the body of the man, and the man is her head. However, the man remains a man, and the woman remains a woman. Similarly, Christ remains God, and the Church remains as humans united with God in a union of love, will, and holiness. "For the husband is the head of the wife even as Christ is the head of the Church, His body, and is Himself its Savior" (Ephesians 5:23).

In the sacrament of marriage, "the two shall become one flesh" (Matthew 19:5). However, the man still has his own body, and so does the woman. The man becomes the head of the woman, and the woman becomes the body of the man. In the same way, the Church becomes the body of Christ, and Christ, with His own body, remains the head of the Church.

7- The body of Christ, united with His divinity, is a living body that we worship, glorify. It performs miracles, and gives us eternal life when we partake of it, "Whoever eats My flesh and drinks My blood has eternal life, and I will raise him up at the last day... so he who feeds on Me will live because of Me" (John 6:54, 57).

As for "the Church, the body of Christ," it does not have divinity, does not give life, and cannot be partaken of. We worship only the head of the Church, "And He is the head of the body, the church, who is the beginning, the firstborn from the dead, that in all things He may have the preeminence" (Colossians 1:18). But we do not worship the Church, for it is us (members of the body). How can we worship ourselves?

8- We are indeed "members of His body, of His flesh and of His bones" (Ephesians 5:30). However, we are not His divinity and hypostasis, just as the woman is the body of the man "bone of my bones and flesh of my flesh" (Genesis 2:23), but she is not the same person as the man. "So we, being many, are one body in Christ, and individually members of one another" (Romans 12:5).

It is in this meaning that our bodies are members of Christ

"Do you not know that your bodies are members of Christ? Shall I then take the members of Christ and make them members of a harlot? Certainly not!" (1 Corinthians 6:15).

"For as the body is one and has many members, but all the members of that one body, being many, are one body, so also is Christ" (1 Corinthians 12:12).

And Christ is the head, "speaking the truth in love, may grow up in all things into Him who is the head—Christ" (Ephesians 4:15).

In conclusion, the sacred Body on the altar is the Body of the Lord Christ, born of the Virgin Mary. It is a sinless and blameless body that unites us to Him when we are baptized in His name and when we partake of Him.

- "For we, though many, are one bread and one body; for we all partake of that one bread" (1 Corinthians 10:17).

- "Make us all worthy, O our Master, to partake of Your holies for the purification of our souls, bodies, and spirits, that we may become one body and one spirit, and may have a share and an inheritance with all the saints who have pleased You since the beginning" (The Basilian Liturgy).

This joining to the body of Christ is now a pledge and an eternity in truth. All of this is by the divine grace granted to humans. This joining to the body of Christ does not give us the attributes of the divine Christ. It is like an electrical device that only works when connected to electricity. But when connected, it does not become electricity; it remains an electrical device and operates with the power of electricity within it. Similarly, we do not live except by Christ, but we do not become Christ; we become Christians, living with the power of Christ's life within us.

The entrance of the lamb into the altar

The altar only receives one offering, and the rest are placed outside the altar, whether before or after the liturgy. The offering that enters the altar symbolizes Christ, who entered the heavenly sanctuary alone. No other offering is placed on the altar except the one representing Christ, chosen from several offerings presented in front of the altar. Therefore, the remaining offerings are placed outside, and none other than Christ, the Lamb, enters. He alone entered the Most Holy Place, "with His own blood He entered the Most Holy Place once for all, having obtained eternal redemption" (Hebrews 9:12).

As for the rest of humanity (the remaining offerings), they remain in paradise or on earth until the general resurrection when we will enter with and in Christ into the Holiest, "Therefore, brethren, having boldness to enter the Holiest by the blood of Jesus" (Hebrews 10:19), "where the forerunner has entered for us, even Jesus, having become High Priest forever according to the order of Melchizedek"(Hebrews 6:20). He himself promised, saying: "I go to prepare a place for you. And if I go and prepare a place for you, I will come again and receive you to Myself; that where I am, there you may be also" (John 14:2-3).

Therefore, only one offering enters the altar and is called "the Lamb." The rest of the offerings remain outside the altar. It is not allowed for any of them to enter the temple before, during, or after the liturgy (let us learn this beautiful lesson). Indeed, "Jesus said to him, 'I am the way, the truth, and the life. No one comes to the Father except through Me'" (John 14:6).

Wiping the offering with water

The priest takes a little water in his right hand and wipes the Lamb placed in his left hand to cleanse it from any impurities, dust, or flour. He wipes it with a little water from above and below, saying, "Grant, O Lord, that our sacrifice may be accepted before You for my own sins and for the ignorance of Your people. For behold, it is pure according to the gift of Your Holy Spirit, in Christ Jesus our Lord".

Now he places his own sins and the ignorance of the people on the head of the Lamb, "Behold, the Lamb of God who takes away the sin of the world" (John 1:29). This is in fulfillment of the ancient Jewish practice: "Aaron shall lay both his hands on the head of the live goat, confess over it all the iniquities of the children of Israel, and all their transgressions, concerning all their sins, putting them on the head of the goat" (Leviticus 16:21).

This is done:

- "That it might be fulfilled which was spoken by Isaiah the prophet, saying: 'He Himself took our infirmities and bore our sicknesses'" (Matthew 8:17).

- "So Christ was offered once to bear the sins of many. To those who eagerly wait for Him, He will appear a second time, apart from sin, for salvation" (Hebrews 9:28).

- "Who Himself bore our sins in His own body on the tree, that we, having died to sins, might live for righteousness—by whose stripes you were healed" (1 Peter 2:24).

Remembrances of the Lamb

The Church considers the water-wiping of the Lamb as a baptism of the Lamb, resembling the baptism of the Lord Jesus by John the Baptist in the Jordan River, where the heavens were opened, "When He had been baptized, Jesus came up immediately from the water; and behold, the heavens were opened to Him, and He saw the Spirit of God descending like a dove and alighting upon Him. And suddenly a voice came from heaven, saying, "This is My beloved Son, in whom I am well pleased."" (Matthew 3:16-17).

Therefore, during the baptism of the Lamb, when the heavens are opened, we seize the opportunity to present our petitions (Remembrances of the Lamb). The priest secretly prays for the living, the departed, the sick, the travellers, the distressed, and for all and for himself. Meanwhile, the congregation chants the Kyrie Eleyson 41 times, seeking mercy, salvation, and participation in the value and effect of the salvific sufferings of the Lord Jesus.

These prayers that the priest inaudibly are called "remembrances of the Lamb." It is a profound opportunity for the priest to place all the burdens of the ministry, the needs of the people, their problems, sighs, and sins on the head of the Lamb, lifting them from him and from them. Many fathers have experienced how problems dissolve and resolve like wax before fire when placed on the Lamb on the altar.

These are God's consolations for His beloved:

"He will fulfill the desire of those who fear Him; He also will hear their cry and save them." (Psalm 145:19).

"But as for me, my prayer is to You, O Lord, in the acceptable time; O God, in the multitude of Your mercy, hear me in the truth of Your salvation" (Psalm 69:13).

"May the Lord fulfill all your petitions" (Psalm 20:5).

"Delight yourself also in the Lord, and He shall give you the desires of your heart" (Psalm 37:4).

And you, my beloved brother, when the voices of the believers rise, crying out, "Kyrie Eleyson, Lord have mercy," at the offering of the lamb, lift your heart with me, crying out, seeking from the Lord forgiveness for your sins and guidance for your needs. He who said, "Call upon Me in the day of trouble; I will deliver you, and you shall glorify Me" (Psalm 50:15). He is the One who promised us to respond, "Before they call, I will answer; and while they are still speaking, I will hear" (Isaiah 65:24). Blessed is he who places his complete hope in God.

Swaddling and Shrouds

After the priest selects the lamb offering and baptizes it with water, he wraps it in a clean and beautiful white cloth. This wrapping signifies the swaddling with which the Lord Jesus was wrapped as a newborn in the manger, "And this will be the sign to you: You will find a Babe wrapped in swaddling cloths, lying in a manger" (Luke 2:12). It also symbolizes the shrouds in which Joseph and Nicodemus wrapped the body of the Lord Jesus after His death, "when Joseph had taken the body, he wrapped it in a clean linen cloth" (Matthew 27:59).

The Lord Christ is present in the liturgy with every detail of His life. He is present as a newborn in the manger, a teacher in the streets of Judea and Galilee, present crucified on the cross on Golgotha, and resurrected and sitting at the right hand of the Father. Moreover, coming in His glory to judge the living and the dead, giving each one according to their deeds, "For as often as you eat this bread and drink the cup, you proclaim the Lord's death until He comes" (1 Corinthians 11:26). "Therefore, as we also commemorate His holy Passion, His Resurrection from the dead, His Ascension into the heavens, His Sitting at Your right hand, O Father, and His Second Coming from the heavens, awesome and full of glory" (Divine Liturgy).

Our Christ transcends time, and His presence in the Eucharist is a real and transcendent presence, surpassing the limits of time. We commemorate not only the past events of His earthly life but also His second coming (which has not yet occurred), acknowledging that He is beyond time and present with all His life events. The paten represents the manger, the cross, the tomb, Mount of Beatitudes, the throne, and the clouds that the Lord Christ will descend upon in His second coming. The cloths represent swaddling, shrouds, and the garment of righteousness in heaven. The prospherine symbolizes the stone which was rolled away from the mouth of the tomb, and the triangular altar cloth above it is the seal of Pilate that sealed the Savior's tomb.

Glory and honor to the Holy Trinity

The priest turns to the west, facing the people, holding the offering in his hands, lifting it wrapped in a cloth in front of his face, proclaiming: "Glory and honor, honor and glory to the Holy Trinity, the Father, the Son, and the Holy Spirit. Peace and edification to the one, holy, catholic, and apostolic Church of God. Amen."

This proclamation is more than a prayer; the priest declares that this liturgy is a glorification and honour to the Holy Trinity, and peace and edification to the Church. If anyone desires to honor our triune God and glorify His holy name, they should participate in the Eucharist. If someone is passionate about edifying the Church and seeks its peace, they should join us in the prayers of the liturgy.

How is the Trinity glorified in the Eucharist?

God is glorified in Himself and doesn't need glory from anyone; creation itself glorifies God without speaking.

- "The heavens declare the glory of God, and the firmament shows His handiwork" (Psalm 19:1).

- "O Lord, how manifold are Your works! In wisdom You have made them all. The earth is full of Your possessions" (Psalm 104:24).

Despite this, God is glorified most in the salvation of humanity, "for the salvation of one human soul is more difficult than the creation of heaven and earth". This is because creation was made by the good and solitary will of God, but the salvation of a human requires the alignment of the human will with God's will, a process that may be hindered by the deviation of human will. "How often I wanted to gather your children together, as a hen gathers her chicks under her wings, but you were not willing!" (Matthew 23:37). The glory of Christ is the cross; it was said of Christ before His crucifixion, "because Jesus was not yet glorified" (John 7:39). Therefore, Jesus said about the hour of His crucifixion, "Father, the hour has come. Glorify Your Son, that Your Son also may glorify You" (John 17:1). Thus, in the liturgy, which is the practical application of the action of the cross, the Holy Trinity is glorified with the salvation of people who participate in prayer and partake of the Lord's Holy Body and Blood.

- "Given for us for salvation, remission of sins, and eternal life to those who partake of Him" (Divine Liturgy).

- "For this is My blood of the new covenant, which is shed for many for the remission of sins" (Matthew 26:28).

Lord Jesus, I want to glorify Your Holy name with Your Good Father and the Holy Spirit. I know that Your glory is through the forgiveness of my sins. Your divine authority to grant me forgiveness reveals Your glory. Therefore, I bow between Your pure hands, asking for pardon and forgiveness. I am confident in Your love and divine power to forgive me, save me, lift away my evil transgressions and my burdensome sins. I am confident that You will give me a new heart that glorifies Your name. When people see me, may they marvel at Your work in me so that I may say with my teacher Paul the Apostle, "and they glorified God in me" (Galatians 1:24), "and all the people, when they saw it, gave praise to God" (Luke 18:43).

I believe that, "where sin abounded, grace abounded much more" (Romans 5:20), so reveal your grace and power in me. Remit, forgive and purify me. Elevate me and elevate my mind from its lowliness and wretchedness. Make me live a life that befits the glory of Your Holy name. Amen

Offering of the Lamb

"Signings of the lamb and the Glory of the Trinity"

After the priest declares that the liturgy is an act of glory for the Holy Trinity, our God, he begins presenting this trinitarian glorification in a practical sense. He faces the altar, and after going around it, he stands before it, and signs the bread and wine three signings, to glorify the Trinity, saying:

During the first signing: "In the name of the Father, the Son, and the Holy Spirit, One God. Blessed be God, the Father the Pantocrator. Amen."

During the second signing: "Blessed is His only-begotten Son, Jesus Christ, our Lord. Amen."

During the third signingl: "Blessed is the Holy Spirit, the Paraclete. Amen."

Accompanying each signing, the deacon responds, saying, "Amen".

The priest concludes the glorification inaudibly, saying: "Glory and honor, honor and glory to the All-Holy Trinity, the Father, and the Son, and the Holy Spirit... Amen", placing the offering in its place on the paten on the altar. Meanwhile, the deacon chants the beautiful melody of "Ispateer" (One is the Holy Father, one is the Holy Son, one is the Holy Spirit). Then, the people respond with the melody of "Thoksa Patri" (Glory to the Father and the Son and the Holy Spirit now and forever and to the ages of ages. Amen). And thus, in a magnificent symphony, the glorification of the Trinity is completed by the priest, the deacon, and the people.

Whoever does not believe in the Trinity will not find a place among us in the liturgy because the liturgy is the glory of the Trinity. And whoever does not glorify the Trinity in prayer is not worthy to partake of the Body of the only-begotten Son at the end of the liturgy. Therefore, we begin our prayers with the glorification of the Trinity, and throughout the prayer, we do not cease to glorify the Holy Trinity. Also, at the end of the liturgy, the priest prays inaudibly, "Establish us in your trinitarian faith until the end."

Oh, the majesty and dignity that surround our holy prayers! We stand before the All-Holy Trinity, speaking to Him and glorifying Him!! The angels stand with all reverence and humility before the divine presence, praising majestically and befittingly, "Above it stood seraphim; each one had six wings: with two he covered his face, with two he covered his feet, and with two he flew. And one cried to another and said: "Holy, holy, holy is the Lord of hosts; The whole earth is full of His glory!" And the posts of the door were shaken by the voice of him who cried out, and the house was filled with smoke." (Isaiah 6:2-4). Truly, "Who is like You, O Lord, among the gods? Who is like You, glorious in holiness, fearful in praises, doing wonders?" (Exodus 15:11).

The fathers praised Him with fear and respect. Hear what Nehemiah says in his holy prayer, "O great and awesome God, You who keep Your covenant and mercy with those who love You and observe Your commandments" (Nehemiah 1:5).

The psalm commands us to worship the Lord with fear:

"Serve the Lord with fear, and rejoice with trembling" (Psalm 2:11).

"But as for me, I will come into Your house in the multitude of Your mercy; In fear of You I will worship toward Your holy temple" (Psalm 5:7).

"For the Lord Most High is awesome; He is a great King over all the earth." (Psalm 47:2).

"O God, You are more awesome than Your holy places. The God of Israel is He who gives strength and power to His people. Blessed be God!" (Psalm 68:35).

"God is greatly to be feared in the assembly of the saints, and to be held in reverence by all those around Him" (Psalm 89:7).

Lord Jesus, how, after all this, can I stand before Your divine presence with indifference and lethargy? How can I praise You with a divided and distracted heart? Or with eyes preoccupied with people or anything distant from You? Or without trembling in the presence of the Trinity!! Let me, my Lord, serve You with the reverence and dignity which befit the holy altar. Let me praise You with joy, reverence and humility, befitting Your holy and glorious presence.

Peace and edification for the Church of God

If the Eucharist is the glorification of the Trinity, it is also the peace of the Church and its edification. Our teacher, the Apostle Paul, spoke about the peace and edification of the Church when he said: "And He Himself gave some to be apostles, some prophets, some evangelists, and some pastors and teachers, for the equipping of the saints for the work of ministry, for the edifying of the body of Christ, till we all come to the unity of the faith and of the knowledge of the Son of God, to a perfect man, to the measure of the stature of the fullness of Christ" (Ephesians 4:11-13).

The Church is the assembly of believers united together in Christ: "So we, being many, are one body in Christ, and individually members of one another" (Romans 12:5).

"For as the body is one and has many members, but all the members of that one body, being many, are one body, so also is Christ" (1 Corinthians 12:12).

"For we are members of His body, of His flesh and of His bones" (Ephesians 5:30).

Edification of the church involves gathering believers and connecting them together in Christ:

"Built on the foundation of the apostles and prophets, Jesus Christ Himself being the chief cornerstone" (Ephesians 2:20).

"You also, as living stones, are being built up a spiritual house, a holy priesthood, to offer up spiritual sacrifices acceptable to God through Jesus Christ" (1 Peter 2:5).

And the Eucharist is the great means to establish us together in Christ. Thust the Church becomes edified, grows and lives in peace.

"Abide in me, and I in you. As the branch cannot bear fruit of itself unless it abides in the vine, so neither can you unless you abide in me" (John 15:4).

"Whoever eats my flesh and drinks my blood abides in me, and I in him" (John 6:56).

"I am the vine, you are the branches. He who abides in me and I in him, he bears much fruit, for apart from me you can do nothing. If anyone does not abide in me, he is thrown away as a branch and dries up, and they gather them and cast them into the fire, and they are burned. If you abide in me, and my words abide in you, ask whatever you wish, and it will be done for you" (John 15:5-7).

This teaching is of ancient in the Church, as we read in the Didascalia (from the 4th century): "Since you are members of Christ, do not open a door to division from the Church by not coming together. Christ is your head, and, according to His promise, He is present among you and a sharer with you. Do not neglect, therefore, your Savior, and do not deprive Him of His members. Do not tear or scatter His body, and do not prefer the concerns of your temporal life to the word of God. But on the day of the Lord, leave everything and hurry together to the Church."

Thus, the Eucharist is the sacrament of the life, persistence and unity of the Church.

This is expressed in one of the ancient prayers in the Apostolic Tradition from the 3rd century AD, "We ask you to send your Holy Spirit upon the offerings of your holy Church, giving unity to all who participate in your sanctities, that they may be filled with the Holy Spirit for the establishment of their faith in the truth."

Lord Jesus, the righteous one, establish me in You so that I may live in You and for You. Without You, I have no life. Gather Your Church and restore the scattered members of Your holy body. Make Your faithful members not neglect to abide in You, by partaking of Your holy Body and precious divine Blood. "Make us all worthy O our Master, to partake of Your Holies, unto the purification of our souls, bodies and spirits, that we may become on body and one spirit, and may have a share and inheritance with all the saints who have pleased You since the beginning".

The third-century martyr Felix said, "Christians celebrate the Eucharist, and the Eucharist establishes Christians. No one can live without the Eucharist."

CHAPTER 5

Thanksgiving Prayer

All liturgical prayers of the church begin with the prayer of thanksgiving.

- At the beginning of the raising of evening and morning incense.

- At the beginning of the Mass after the presentation of the oblation.

- At the beginning of the consecration of the oils.

- At the beginning of funeral prayers, unction of the sick and blessing of the waters

- At the beginning of Pascha Prayers

- In the prayers over the baptismal waters

- In the prayers of matrimony

- At the beginning of each of the hours of the Agpeya

In general, we give thanks at the beginning of all prayers. "I thank my God always concerning you for the grace of God which was given to you by Christ Jesus" (1 Corinthians 1:4).

The Scriptures teach us that gratitude is the gateway to a relationship with God. "Be anxious for nothing, but in everything by prayer and supplication, with thanksgiving, let your requests be made known to God" (Philippians 4:6). They also teach us to be persistent in thanksgiving. "Continue earnestly in prayer, being vigilant in it with thanksgiving" (Colossians 4:2). "For this reason we also thank God without ceasing" (1 Thessalonians 2:13) and "in everything give thanks; for this is the will of God in Christ Jesus for you." (1 Thessalonians 5:18).

Gratitude, according to the Holy Scriptures, is considered a pleasing service to God. Therefore, since we are receiving a kingdom that cannot be shaken, let us be thankful, and so worship God acceptably with reverence and awe"" (Hebrews 12:28)[1].

The angels and heavenly forces never cease to give thanks to God in heaven.

"Whenever the living creatures give glory and honor and thanks to Him who sits on the throne, who lives forever and ever" (Revelation 4:9). "Saying "Amen! Blessing and glory and wisdom, thanksgiving and honor and power and might, be to our God forever and ever. Amen"" (Revelation 7:12). "We give You thanks, O Lord God Almighty, the One who is and who was and who is to come, because You have taken Your great power and reigned" (Revelation 11:17).

Therefore, we should be "giving thanks to the Father who has qualified us to be partakers of the inheritance of the saints in the light" (Colossians 1:12), "being thankful" (Colossians 3:15), and "whatever [we] do in word or deed, do all in the name of the Lord Jesus, giving thanks to God the Father through Him" (Colossians 3:17).

The Meaning of Thanksgiving:

Thanksgiving means accepting grace, and the Coptic word "Shepehmot" carries this meaning. "Shep" means "to accept," and "ehmot" means "grace." In Greek, the word for thanksgiving is "Evcharistia," which has the same meaning. "Ev" means "good," and "charis" means "grace." Thus, in giving thanks, we acknowledge

---

[1] The NIV translation was used here as NKJV uses "let us have grace" where NIV translates "let us be thankful". The Arabic translation uses a word meaning "thankful", and given this is a chapter on thanksgiving, NIV was used to preserve the intent. Note: the Greek is which can be translated as either grace or gratitude (grace on the part of the doer, or gratitude on the part of the receiver).

Thanksgiving Prayer

God's grace as good and great, accepting it with gratitude and thanks.

This meaning is present in the opening statement of the Tertullus in his speech with Governor Felix, recorded in the Acts, where he said: "Seeing that through you we enjoy great peace, and prosperity is being brought to this nation by your foresight, we accept it always and in all places, most noble Felix, with all thankfulness." (Acts 24:2-3).

The relationship between God and humanity revolves around this dual axis. "God does not cease to give us grace, and we should not cease to accept His grace, meaning we should not cease to thank Him."

The ancient fathers said, "There is no gift without increase except that which is without thanks." Therefore, we thank Him in every occasion in every condition and for all things, and do not cease to give thanks, "giving thanks always for all things to God the Father in the name of our Lord Jesus Christ" (Ephesians 5:20).

In the prayer of thanksgiving, we confess that God is the beneficent, "He has made everything beautiful in its time. Also He has put eternity in their hearts, except that no one can find out the work that God does from beginning to end." (Ecclesiastes 3:11). Indeed, He turns the evil plans of the devil and wicked people into good for His beloved children. "And we know that all things work together for good to those who love God, to those who are the called according to His purpose" (Romans 8:28). Just as He did with Joseph the righteous, turning his brothers' plot for evil into good. "But as for you, you meant evil against me; but God meant it for good, in order to bring it about as it is this day, to save many people alive" (Genesis 50:20).

We believe that we are in the faithful hands God, which bestow upon us goodness. We also believe that God is "merciful." "And the Lord passed before him and proclaimed, "The Lord, the Lord God, merciful and gracious, longsuffering, and abounding in goodness and truth" (Exodus 34:6). "(for the Lord your God is a merciful God), He will not forsake you nor destroy you, nor forget the covenant of your fathers which He swore to them" (Deuteronomy 4:31). "But You, O Lord, are a God full of compassion, and gracious, Longsuffering and abundant in mercy and truth" (Psalm 86:15). "The Lord is gracious and full of compassion, slow to anger and great in mercy." (Psalms 145:8)

We also cannot live without the mercy and compassion of God upon us, and without this mercy, we would have perished from the beginning. "Unless the Lord of hosts Had left to us a very small remnant, we would have become like Sodom, we would have been made like Gomorrah" (Isaiah 1:9).

We thank our merciful God because He "covered us". Truly, "The beloved of the Lord shall dwell in safety by Him, who shelters him all the day long; and he shall dwell between His shoulders" (Deuteronomy 33:12). He covers our weaknesses and neglects. "For in the time of trouble He shall hide me in His pavilion; in the secret place of His tabernacle He shall hide me; He shall set me high upon a rock" (Psalm 27:5). And He covers us from the evil of evildoers. "You shall hide them in the secret place of Your presence from the plots of man; You shall keep them secretly in a pavilion From the strife of tongues" (Psalm 31:20). He also covers our sins and forgives them for us. "Blessed is he whose transgression is forgiven, whose sin is covered" (Psalm 32:1). He covers us in times of distress. "You are my hiding place; You shall preserve me from trouble; You shall surround me with songs of deliverance" (Psalm 32:7).

"Helped us"… May God assist us in our weakness and strengthen us with His power. "Behold, God is my helper; The Lord is with those who uphold my life." (Psalm 54:4). Without this divine assistance, we would falter, and our eternity would be lost. "Unless the Lord had been my help, my soul would soon have settled in silence" (Psalm 94:17). Truly, "Happy is he who has the God of Jacob for his help, whose hope is in the Lord his God," (Psalm 146:5). Therefore, we are reassured because the Lord is our helper. "So we may boldly say: The Lord is my helper; I will not fear. What can man do to me"." (Hebrews 13:6)."

"Preserved us"… May God preserve His children from all evil. "You who love the Lord, hate evil! He preserves the souls of His saints;

He delivers them out of the hand of the wicked" (Psalm 97:10). "The Lord preserves the simple" (Psalm 116:6). "He will not allow your foot to be moved; He who keeps you will not slumber. Behold, He who keeps Israel Shall neither slumber nor sleep. The Lord is your keeper; The Lord is your shade at your right hand" (Psalm 121:3-5).

"Accepted us to Himself"… It is out of God's goodness that He does not reject us despite our sins and transgressions. Despite the trials and rebellions that the people of Israel faced, He says of them, "He has not observed iniquity in Jacob, nor has He seen wickedness in Israel. The Lord his God is with him, And the shout of a King is among them" (Numbers 23:21). He says to the virgin in the Song of Songs (symbolic of each of our souls): "You are all fair, my love, And there is no spot in you" (Song of Solomon 4:7).

"Had compassion "… He is a loving Father who shows compassion to His children. "Behold, I will extend peace to her like a river, And the glory of the Gentiles like a flowing stream. Then you shall feed; On her sides shall you be carried, and be dandled on her knees" (Isaiah 66:12). "As one whom his mother comforts, so I will comfort you; you shall be comforted in Jerusalem" (Isaiah 66:13). "He will feed His flock like a shepherd; He will gather the lambs with His arm, And carry them in His bosom, And gently lead those who are with young" (Isaiah 40:11).

"Supported us"… That is, helped us in all matters of our spiritual and social lives. Truly, there is no one to support us in our difficulties and hardships except Him.

"Brought us to this hour "… Also, among God's kindness is that He grants us life and a new day. "Through the Lord's mercies we are not consumed, because His compassions fail not" (Lamentations 3:22).

"Grant us to complete this blessed day and all the days of our lives in peace, with Your fear".. We ask you to give us your peace that surpasses all understanding. "And the peace of God, which surpasses all understanding, will guard your hearts and your minds in Christ Jesus" (Philippians 4:7).

While enjoying God's peace, we should not lose sight of His great reverence. Truly, "Who is like You, O Lord, among the gods? Who is like You, glorious in holiness, fearful in praises, doing wonders?" (Exodus 15:11). " For the Lord Most High is awesome; He is a great King over all the earth." (Psalm 47:2). "O God, You are more awesome than Your holy places. The God of Israel is He who gives strength and power to His people. Blessed be God!" (Psalm 68:35). "God is greatly to be feared in the assembly of the saints, and to be held in reverence by all those around Him." (Psalm 89:7).

The fatherhood of God does not diminish His majesty and awe. Moses spoke to "the Lord… face to face, as a man speaks to his friend" (Exodus 33:11). Moses, the archprophet, said, "I am exceedingly afraid and trembling" (Hebrews 12:21), when he met God on the mountain that burned with fire.

"All envy, all temptation, all works of Satan"… The devil, the enemy of all good, does not rest in the face of the success of God's children. He begins to plot problems for them with great envy and tests them with cruelty, but our God protects us from his evil and harm. Sin and death entered into the world through the envy of the devil. "But through the devil's envy death entered the world" (Wisdom 2:24). Satan dared and fought against the Lord Christ Himself on the mountain, the enemy who sows tares among the wheat, the one who takes away the word from the hearts of the hearers. "And give no opportunity to the devil" (Ephesians 4:27). Therefore, we must resist the devil. "Put on the whole armor of God, that you may be able to stand against the wiles of the devil" (Ephesians 6:11). "Therefore submit to God. Resist the devil and he will flee from you." (James 4:7). "Be sober, be vigilant; because your adversary the devil walks about like a roaring lion, seeking whom he may devour" (1 Peter 5:8).

"All intrigues of the wicked".. The evil that has overcome people leads them to devise plots and conspiracies against the children of God. Our teacher, the Apostle Paul, suffered from such plots. "serving the Lord with all humility, with many tears and trials which happened to me by the plotting of the Jews" (Acts 20:19). "Yet in all these things we are more than conquerors through Him who loved us" (Romans 8:37).

"And the rising up of enemies, seen and unseen".. The visible enemies are known, but who are the hidden enemies? My enemy might be my own body, leading me to sin. It could be stumbling friends, or people feigning love while harboring enmity. In general, we pray that Christ, our God, will protect us from the evils of both visible and hidden enemies.

"But those things which are good and profitable do provide for us"... What we do must be good and beneficial. Every plan, every word, and every action must be done with God. "But he who does the truth comes to the light, that his deeds may be clearly seen, that they have been done in God" (John 3:21).

"For it is you who has given us the authority to trample on serpents and scorpions, an dover all the power of the enemy"... "Behold, I give you the authority to trample on serpents and scorpions, and over all the power of the enemy, and nothing shall by any means hurt you" (Luke 10:19).

Serpents and scorpions are Satan and his forces, and Christ has conquered them for our sake. "I saw Satan fall like lightning from heaven" (Luke 10:18). "And do not lead us into temptation, but deliver us from the evil one." (Luke 11:4), "No evil will befall the one who fears the Lord, but in trials such a one will be rescued again and again." (Sirach 33:1)

Satan does not cease to tempt the children of God. "My child, when you come to serve the Lord, prepare yourself for testing. Set your heart right and be steadfast, and do not be impetuous in time of calamity." (Sirach 2:1-2).

Our Father Abraham overcame temptation: "Was not Abraham found faithful when tested, and it was reckoned to him as righteousness?" (1 Maccabees 2:52). Therefore, Christ advised us: "Watch and pray, lest you enter into temptation. The spirit indeed is willing, but the flesh is weak" (Mark 14:38).

And God does not abandon us in our trials. "but with the temptation will also make the way of escape, that you may be able to bear it." (1 Corinthians 10:13). "the Lord knows how to deliver the godly out of temptations and to reserve the unjust under punishment for the day of judgment" (2 Peter 2:9). "Because you have kept My command to persevere, I also will keep you from the hour of trial which shall come upon the whole world, to test those who dwell on the earth." (Revelation 3:10).

Therefore, we do not fear trials but rejoice in them. "My brethren, count it all joy when you fall into various trials" (James 1:2).

CHAPTER 6

The Covering

After the prayer of thanksgiving, the priest covers the altar with the Prospherin after placing the offering in the paten and covering it with an altar cloth. Similarly, the wine and water in the chalice are covered with an altar cloth. During this time, the inaudible prayer of the Prothesis or the covering is prayed. The altar remains covered, until the end of the prayer of reconciliation.

Why do we cover the sacrifice?

1. This covering indicates that a significant part of the life of the Lord Jesus on earth was hidden. We know nothing about the life of the Lord Jesus from His birth until His baptism, except for the account that our teacher Luke narrated when the Lord Jesus was 12 years old.

The life of the Lord Jesus is a holiness that cannot be approached. "All things have been delivered to Me by My Father, and no one knows the Son except the Father. Nor does anyone know the Father except the Son, and the one to whom the Son wills to reveal Him." (Matthew 11:27).

2. Also, the personality of the Lord Jesus, not just His life, is a puzzle that bewilders minds, a hidden treasure of knowledge revealed only in a few words. No matter what we know about Him, we are told, "And if anyone thinks that he knows anything, he knows nothing

yet as he ought to know." (1 Cor 8:2). Therefore, none of us can fully trust in his knowledge; we are still growing in the knowledge of God, which is "eternal life" (John 17:3).

3. Also, covering the sacrifice indicates the period of the burial of the Savior in the tomb, which ended with the resurrection from the dead (lifting the Prospherin after the prayer of reconciliation).

4. The divinity of the Lord Jesus was veiled and not clearly announced except by the resurrection from the dead. That is why our teacher Paul the Apostle said about Him, "Concerning His Son Jesus Christ our Lord, who was born of the seed of David according to the flesh and declared to be the Son of God with power according to the Spirit of holiness, by the resurrection from the dead." (Rom 1:3-4).

Therefore, after the prayer of reconciliation, which corresponds to the resurrection of Christ in the events of His holy life, the priest lifts the Prospherin and shakes it, indicating the earthquake that accompanied the announcement of the resurrection of the Savior. After that, the Holy Sacrifice is revealed, as if saying: We have seen Him and known Him in the resurrection. The holy resurrection has declared to us that He is the Son of God in truth.

Offering Vessels

"O Master Lord Jesus Christ, the co-eternal Logos" (i.e. a partner in the same divine essence as the Father and the Holy Spirit). "who is of one essence with Him and the Holy Spirit. You are the living bread which came down from heaven." We are about to undertake the mystery of this sacred bread, giving life to the world, according to the words of the Lord Jesus:

"For the bread of God is He who comes down from heaven and gives life to the world." (John 6:33).

"And Jesus said to them, "I am the bread of life. He who comes to Me shall never hunger, and he who believes in Me shall never thirst." (John 6:35).

"This is the bread which comes down from heaven, that one may eat of it and not die" (John 6:50)

"I am the living bread which came down from heaven. If anyone eats of this bread, he will live forever; and the bread that I shall give is My flesh, which I shall give for the life of the world" (John 6:51)

"This is the bread which came down from heaven—not as your fathers ate the manna, and are dead. He who eats this bread will live forever." (John 6:58).

The Lord Jesus chose to become bread for us to eat, to unite with Him and obtain life through Him. "and formerly made Yourself a lamb without spot for the life of the world"

Have you seen a greater wonder than this? For the shepherd to become a lamb amid His sheep? And for the Vinedresser the Son of the Vine dresser (the sower), the vine? And for the true God begotten of the true God to become human? Have you seen a greater love and care than this?

He became a lamb without blemish amid the lambs to lead them to fertile pastures safely, making them feel His friendship and closeness. Thus, John the Baptist testified about him, saying: "The next day John saw Jesus coming toward him, and said, "Behold! The Lamb of God who takes away the sin of the world! (John 1:29). Also, Saint Peter the Apostle taught us that we were redeemed "but with the precious blood of Christ, as of a lamb without blemish and without spot." (1 Peter 1:19).

"Show Your face upon this bread, and upon this cup…in order that… this bread may indeed become Your holy Body… and the mixture which is in this cup indeed Your precious Blood" These are the beginning words of the consecration prayers prayed by the priest in preparation for the descent of the Holy Spirit in the later parts of the liturgy when he signs the cross with his hand on the offering in the paten three signs quickly, saying, "And this bread makes it a holy Body for Him," then three more signs quickly on the cup, saying, "And this cup a Precious blood for the new covenant."

When the priest utters the word "Body," the bread, by the action of the Holy Spirit, transforms into the real body of our Lord Jesus Christ, our God. And when he utters the word "Blood," the mixture in the chalice transforms into the real Blood of our Lord Jesus Christ, our God. Therefore, the rite emphasizes that the priest should quickly sign the bread (before the transformation) while the priest can still sign, as he does not dare to sign the Body of Christ (after the transformation), and the same goes for the chalice

All of this is by the action of the Holy Spirit and does not depend on the priest's righteousness or his spirituality or his priestly rank. It is sufficient that the priest be an ordained (decreed) priest with proper ordination by laying hands from a bishop holding a valid priesthood.

The priest prays the litany of the descent of the Holy Spirit while prostrating, and all the people prostrate, seeking the descent of the Holy Spirit upon them and the offerings placed on the altar. "purify them, change them (transform them), and manifest them as a sanctification of Your saints."

Back to the Prothesis Sacrament:

In the Prothesis Sacrament, the priest recites the first words of sanctification and transformation: "show Your face upon this bread and upon this cup." This transformation is done by the Holy Spirit according to the promise of Christ and His inexpressible gift. "May they become for all of us communion, healing, and salvation for our souls, bodies and spirits". Whoever unites with Christ our God in the sacrament of the Eucharist ascends and is healed from sin and saved, for He is "given for the remission of sins and eternal life to those who partake of Him."

CHAPTER 7

The Absolution

After the Prothesis sacrament, the priest prays (inaudibly) the same absolution that be prays over the confessor after the sacrament of confession. Thereby, the Church prays this absolution once for each person after confession, and again for the entire congregation to achieve collective salvation with collective repentance. Then all the altar servants exit the altar and prostrate themselves before its entrance, and the priest prays the absolution of the servants over them, making them ready to serve these holy mysteries.

In this absolution, it is noted that the people are considered among the servants of the liturgy, "May Your servants, ministers of this day, the hegumens, the priests, the deacons, the clergy, and all the people...". Thus, the people are accounted for in the conscience of the Church as servants of the sacraments, actively participating in the sanctification of the mysteries rather than being mere observers and listeners.

The names of the saints mentioned in the absolution are the names of fathers who hold a rank of priesthood, giving them the right to offer absolution. For example, the names of female saints are not mentioned, including our Lady, the Virgin Mary, as there is no priesthood for women. Similarly, the names of the great martyrs who were not priests, such as Saint George, Saint Mena, and Saint Philopateer Mercurius, are not mentioned.

The fathers mentioned in this absolution are the champions of Orthodoxy who excommunicated the heretics and expelled them from the company of the Church due to their doctrinal deviations. We mention them in the absolution of the servants to affirm our Orthodoxy, our submission to the Orthodox fathers, and our commitment to their path in preserving the faith, adhering to it, and not deviating from it.

In the absolution of the servants, we take absolution from:

1. The Holy Trinity: because our faith is a Trinitarian faith. We believe in the Father, the Son, and the Holy Spirit, the Trinity equal in essence and distinct in hypostases.

2. The Universal Church: because we are its members through baptism, and we have not lost this membership because we have not shared in the sins of the heretics.

3. From the mouth of the Apostolic Fathers: because our faith is apostolic, "built on the foundation of the apostles and prophets, with Christ Jesus Himself as the chief cornerstone" (Ephesians 2:20). We received this faith accurately and did not neglect to preserve it based on their holy command: "To contend earnestly for the faith which was once for all delivered to the saints" (Jude 1:3).

4. From the mouth of Saint Mark the Apostle: the carrier of the Gospel to our Egyptian land, who brought us the light of faith. Every member of the great Church he established is called to continue in the same Markian faith and not deviate from it.

5. The Fathers: Cyril, Dioscorus, Athanasius, Peter, Chrysostom, Cyril, Basil, Gregory… who fought against the heretics. We can only pray if we take absolution from their pure mouths. They also do not give absolution except to those who believe in the same faith they defended vigorously.

6. And the fathers of the three councils: Nicaea, Constantinople, and Ephesus. These councils are considered by our Coptic Church to be legitimate and Orthodox, where heretics such as Arius, Macedonius, Nestorius, and Sabellius, were excommunicated. Whoever attends the liturgy and seeks absolution from the mouths of the fathers of these councils declares that they do not agree with the heretical opinions of these evildoers.

7. From the mouth of His Holiness the Pope, and the bishops of the diocese. This declares that the priest and the entire people, as well as all the clergy, submit to the fatherhood and leadership of the Pope of the Church and its bishop. They do not pray alone without receiving absolution from their pure mouths. The Church is one and does not divide, and the sign of this unity is the submission of all to the one bishop of the diocese. Submission is in committing to the same faith and the same Orthodox teaching that the bishop holds.

CHAPTER

8

Liturgy of the Word

After the procession, the thanksgiving prayer, and the servants' absolution, a section in the Divine Liturgy begins, known as the Liturgy of the Catechumens.

Who are the Catechumens?

They are people who believe in the Lord Jesus Christ but have not yet been baptized. The Church takes its time in baptizing adults to ensure the validity and sincerity of their faith. The Church allows them to attend a portion of the liturgy to join in prayer, listen to the readings and sermon, recite the Christian creed, and then they leave. They are not allowed to attend the Liturgy of the Eucharist or witness the sacred mysteries until they are baptized in the name of the Trinity. As for children, they are baptized without delay, based on the faith of their parents.

Baptism of Children

The Apostle Paul considered the crossing of the Red Sea by the people of God as a baptism for them. "I do not want you to be unaware that all our fathers were under the cloud, all passed through the sea, all were baptized into Moses in the cloud and in the sea" (1 Corinthians 10:1-2). This crossing of the sea was due to the people believing in the word of God through the prophet Moses, crossing while trusting in God's power to save them. "By faith they passed through the Red Sea as by dry land, whereas the Egyptians, attempting to do so, were drowned" (Hebrews 11:29). Children, on the other hand, cross in the hands of their parents, without examination or discussion, but based on the faith of their parents. The verse "He who believes and is baptized will be saved" (Mark 16:16) applies to adult baptism, while for children, the words of our Lord Jesus apply, "Let the little children come to Me, and do not forbid them; for of such is the kingdom of God" (Mark 10:14). St Philip told the Ethiopian Eunuch that he must be a believer to baptise him; when the eunuch asked him, "" See, here is water. What hinders me from being baptized?" Then Philip said, "If you believe with all your heart, you may." And he answered and said, "I believe that Jesus Christ is the Son of God"" (Acts 8:36-37). Likewise, Paul and Silas stipulated that the prison keeper in Philippi believe that he may be saved, ""Sirs, what must I do to be saved?" So they said, "Believe on the Lord Jesus Christ, and you will be saved, you and your household"" (Acts 16:30-31). Thus, because of his faith "he and all his family were baptized" (Acts 16:33).

Our teacher Paul also considered circumcision in the Old Testament as a symbol of baptism in the New Testament. He said, "In Him you were also circumcised with the circumcision made without hands, by putting off the body of the sins of the flesh, by the circumcision of Christ, buried with Him in baptism, in which you also were raised with Him through faith in the working of God, who raised Him from the dead" (Colossians 2:11-12).

Circumcision was a sign of the covenant and entry into the care of God's people, and similarly, baptism is the secret to entering into the membership of the body of Christ. If man, in the Old Testament, accepted circumcision as an eight-day-old child, how much more fitting is it for a child to accept baptism in the New Covenant, to enjoy early membership in the body of Christ and the grace of God, which is not limited by righteousness or knowledge or age of the person.

Liturgy of the Word

Why is it called the "Liturgy of the Catechumens"?

This part of the liturgy is named not because it is limited to the catechumens but because only the catechumens were allowed to attend this part. It begins after the offering of the lamb and extends to the end of the sermon and the prayers after the Gospel and the Nicene Creed.

This part includes hymns, melodies, prayers, readings, and teachings. Christian faith is transmitted to the catechumens not only through reading and teaching but also through prayer and praise. Even the reading of the sacred texts in the liturgy is done with a simple melody to express that reading the Holy Scriptures is also a form of prayer and praise. These melodies help the reader and the listener focus on the words and their meanings. (These melodies were used in reading the epistles and acts in the Coptic language. However, in translation, readings are done without melodies, but the use of melody continues in reading the Psalms and the Gospel in Coptic and Arabic).

Ecclesiastical Readings

The practice of reading the holy books in the church during the liturgy dates back to the apostolic age. Information about this practice is mentioned in the letter of the Apostle Paul to the Colossians: "Now when this epistle is read among you, see that it is read also in the church of the Laodiceans, and that you likewise read the epistle from Laodicea" (Colossians 4:16).

The second-century saint Justin Martyr said, "It is the custom of Christians to gather together on Sunday for worship, to read the apostles' writings and the prophets' sayings." Tertullian, also from the second century, said, "On Sunday, Christians gather to read the sacred books and sing Psalms."

The daily reading includes:

1- Vespers: Psalm and Gospel.

2- Matins: Psalm and Gospel.

3- Divine Liturgy: Pauline (a chapter from the letters of our teacher, the Apostle Paul), and Catholicon (a chapter from the Catholic Epistles - James, Peter, John, Jude), and the Praxis (a chapter from the Acts of the Apostles). Then the Synaxarium, which contains the biography of the saint of the day, followed by the Agios chant and the Psalm and Gospel of the Liturgy.

All these readings serve the same purpose that corresponds to the day, whether it is a feast day, a commemoration of a saint, a fasting day, or one of the annual Sundays, etc

The Katameros

The book that contains selected chapters from the Holy Bible for reading in the Divine Liturgy is called the Katameros. This word is of Greek origin, consisting of two parts: "kata," meaning "according to," and "meros" meaning "days". It is a book arranged according to the days.

In our Coptic Church, there are five types of Katameros:

1- Annual Katameros: Used throughout the Coptic year, except for days when other types of Katameros are used, as will be explained later. The Annual Katameros arranges the readings according to the Church's celebration of the saint of the day.

For example, the readings for the feast of the Holy Virgin Mary explain matters specific to her and her symbols in the Holy Scripture. The readings for the feasts of the angels explain the nature of their service to us. Likewise, the readings for the feasts of the apostles, martyrs, patriarchs, or fathers who defended the Orthodox faith, and so on.

2- Sunday Katameros: Used on Sundays throughout the year, except during the Great Lent and the Fifty Days. The readings are arranged in a special way, explaining the work of the Holy Trinity in the economy of salvation for humanity.

3- Great Lent Katameros: Used during the days and Sundays of the Great Holy Lent, up to Lazarus Saturday. Its readings aim to prepare the catechumens for baptism by explaining the effects of this sacred sacrament. Also, it aims to direct the minds of believers to repentance, returning to the covenant of holy baptism. The Great Lent Katameros is distinctive for including selected chapters from the Old Testament (the Prophets), recited during the raising of morning incense before the Gospel, in addition to the regular readings from the New Testament.

4- Holy Pascha Katameros: Used during Holy Week, from Lazarus Saturday to the glorious Resurrection feast. In it, the Church follows the Lord Jesus Christ step by step in His last week on earth. The Holy Pascha Katameros includes special arrangements that are entirely different from the regular Katameros. The focus is entirely on the sufferings of the Lord Jesus Christ, through prophecies, Psalms, and Gospels.

5- Fifty Days Katameros: Used in the period between the glorious Resurrection and the Feast of Pentecost (the descent of the Holy Spirit on the fiftieth day after the Resurrection). The readings of the Fifty Days focus on proving the divinity of the Lord Jesus Christ, as His divinity was clearly proclaimed by the holy Resurrection. As our teacher, the Apostle Paul, explained: "And declared to be the Son of God with power according to the Spirit of holiness, by the resurrection from the dead" (Romans 1:4). The Fifty Days Katameros also reviews how we live in Christ through the Eucharist and how the Lord Jesus Christ is for us the Bread of Life, the Living Water, and the True Light.

Prayers During the Readings

During the reading of the Pauline, Catholicon, and the Praxis, the priest prays very deep inaudible prayers while censing. The purpose of these prayers is for God to open the hearts of the listeners to understand what the Spirit is saying to the churches.

"Consider what I say, and may the Lord give you understanding in all things" (2 Timothy 2:7).

"And He opened their understanding, that they might comprehend the Scriptures" (Luke 24:45).

We are in desperate need for the Lord to open the eyes of our hearts to understand His eternal divine purposes when we read or hear chapters from the Holy Scriptures, "in which are some things hard to understand" (2 Peter 3:16). Therefore, the priest prays in the inaudible prayer of the Pauline: "be with us also, O our Master, in this hour, and stand in the midst of us all." "O Lord of knowledge and provider of wisdom who reveals the deep things (what is deep and obscure in the spiritual meanings of the Holy Scriptures), and the one who gives a word to those who preach with great power... We ask you to grant us and all your people, a mind free from wondering and a clear understanding that we may know and understand how profitable are Your holy teachings which are now read to us through him (Paul the Apostle). Make us resemble him in action and faith..."

In the inaudible prayer of the Catholic Epistle, the priest also says: "O Lord, our God, who through Your holy apostles has revealed to us the mystery of the Gospel of the glory of Your Christ... that they should proclaim among all nations the glad tidings of the unsearchable riches of Your mercy... make us worthy of their share and inheritance. Grant us at all times to walk in their footsteps and to imitate their struggle, and to have communion with them in the sweat which they accepted for the sake of godliness (the sweat they shed as they strive to spread the Gospel with piety)".

Note here that prayer does not focus only on mental understanding but on practical application (their footsteps, struggles, efforts, piety)...

"Remember those who rule over you, who have spoken the word of God to you, whose faith follow, considering the outcome of their conduct" (Hebrews 13:7).

"Remind them of these things, charging them before the Lord not to strive about words to no profit, to the ruin of the hearers. (2 Timothy 2:14).

"But be doers of the word, and not hearers only, deceiving yourselves" (James 1:22).

For "Not everyone who says to Me, 'Lord, Lord,' shall enter the kingdom of heaven, but he who does the will of My Father in heaven" (Matthew 7:21).

"Blessed are those who hear the word of God and keep it" (Luke 11:28).

The Sanctifying Action of Readings

The sacred readings in the liturgy are not only for teaching but also for sanctification. In this regard, Bishop Severus of Ashmunein from the 10th century AD says, "The books and the liturgy were established before the offering to sanctify the believer's soul and body, purify it, and then the offering becomes deserved." Therefore, listening to church readings is a significant qualification for partaking in the holy mysteries.

This is also a biblical teaching, "It is sanctified by the word of God and prayer" (1 Timothy 4:5). Both the word of God and prayer sanctify offerings and individuals.

Therefore, we must honor attending the church early to avoid missing this crucial part of our preparation for communion. We should also listen carefully, attentively and prayerfully to the sacred readings.

This also requires the reader of the Scripture to be skilled in reading, understanding the meaning of what is reading, mastering it, reading Arabic with proper pronunciation, clear articulation of letters and words, and audible voice not too faint and not too loud, "So likewise you, unless you utter by the tongue words easy to understand, how will it known what is spoken? For you will be speaking into the air." (1 Corinthians 14:9).

The Synaxarion

After reading the Synaxarium, which contains stories and lives of saints for us to learn from, according to the scripture "Remember those who rule over you, who have spoken the word of God to you, whose faith follow, considering the outcome of their conduct" (Hebrews 13:7). After this sacred reading, a brief glorification of the saint of the day is performed because God is "glorified in them" (John 17:10), and He glorifies them... "And the glory which You gave Me I have given them" (John 17:22).

We know that God is the Holy One of the hollies. Therefore, after glorifying them, we lift up the sanctification to Christ our God, from whom all holiness, glory, and honor are derived, and we glorify Him with the hymn "Agios."

When people praise you, lift your eyes to the sky,

and glorify the name of Christ, who covered your weaknesses,

to the point that people only see in you what they praise you for.

And when you hear about human glories, give them their right in glory and honor,

but do not forget that God is the source of all inspiration, creativity, and intellectual works.

So, elevate your mind with glorification to God for His sacred creation.

Agios Hymn

In the Agios hymn, we praise the hypostasis of the Son, saying to Him, "Holy God, Holy Mighty, Holy Immortal, who was born of the Virgin, have mercy on us. Holy God, Holy Mighty, Holy Immortal, who was crucified for us, have mercy on us. Holy God, Holy Mighty, Holy Immortal, who rose from the dead and ascended to the heavens, have mercy on us." This hymn is taken from the one Isaiah the Prophet saw, "And this one cried and said: 'Holy, Holy,

Holy is the Lord of hosts. The whole earth is full of His glory'" (Isaiah 6:3). The fourth-century saint Cyril of Jerusalem said about this hymn, "As we chant this theological hymn that we received about the seraphim, we share the heavenly hosts in the praise of thanksgiving."

We pray this hymn without melody in the Agpeya prayers in Vespers and Matins, and in the raising of Evening and Morning incense before the chanting of the Doxologies. It is also said in its distinctive melody in the Liturgy of the Faithful before the litany of the Gospel.

"Holy God"… truly "No one is holy like the Lord, for there is none besides You" (1 Samuel 2:2), and He wants us to be holy like Him. "For I am the Lord your God. You shall therefore consecrate yourselves, and you shall be holy; for I am holy" (Leviticus 11:44). Because He is holy, He finds rest in holy souls.

The Psalms teach us to sing about the holiness of the Lord:

"But You are holy, Enthroned in the praises of Israel" (Psalm 22:3).

"For our heart shall rejoice in Him, Because we have trusted in His holy name" (Psalm 33:21).

"Also with the lute I will praise You— And Your faithfulness, O my God! To You I will sing with the harp, O Holy One of Israel" (Psalm 71:22).

"Let them praise Your great and awesome name—He is holy." (Psalm 99:3).

"Exalt the Lord our God, And worship at His holy hill; For the Lord our God is holy." (Psalm 99:9).

"Bless the Lord, O my soul, and all that is within me, bless His holy name" (Psalm 103:1).

"Glory is His holy name; Let the heart of those rejoice who seek the Lord!" Psalm 105:3

"My mouth shall speak the praise of the Lord, and all flesh shall bless His holy name Forever and ever" Psalm 154:21

Reflections on the Agios hymn:

"Holy Mighty"... God is powerful and capable of everything... "But You are my strong refuge" (Psalm 71:7). "And the prayer of Nehemiah was held in this way: O' Lord, creator of all, feared and powerful, just and merciful, you alone are the king and the righteous" (2 Maccabees 1:24). And we draw strength from and seek refuge in this power... "The Lord is my strength and my song, and He has become my salvation. He is my God, and I will praise Him; my father's God, and I will exalt Him" (Exodus 15:2).

"Holy immortal"... God is immortal, meaning He is not subject to death... "Who alone has immortality, dwelling in unapproachable light" (1 Timothy 6:16). "For with You is the fountain of life" (Psalm 36:9), "In Him was life, and the life was the light of men" (John 1:4).

Our God... the Holy Mighty Living One who is not subject to death... accepted for our sake and for our salvation to incarnate, be born of a woman, be crucified for us, and rise from the dead on the third day. This is what we glorify Him for in this magnificent hymn, as if we are saying: Does it make sense that the unlimited God becomes a limited human? Can the incomprehensible become tangible, and the eternal be temporal Does it make sense that the immortal dies and rises again?

The answer to all these questions is contained in two truths:

1. "God Almighty" (Genesis 48:3).

2. "Because the Lord loves you, and because He would keep the oath which He swore to your fathers" (Deuteronomy 7:8).

God is capable of all things, and His extreme love for humanity makes Him accept everything for our sake. As we chant in the hymn (Omonogenis) on Good Friday: "Holy God, who being God (did not lose His divinity), for our sake, became man without change (without alteration)".

"Holy Mighty who by weakness (death, pain, and humiliation) showed forth what is greater than power (salvation, victory over Satan, death and sin)."

"Holy immortal, who was crucified for our sake, and endured death in His flesh, the Eternal and Immortal". He endured this unbefitting situation temporarily because He will definitely rise again "having loosed the pains of death, because it was not possible that He should be held by it" (Acts 2:24).

Truly, our loving God worked the impossible for us and for our salvation. Therefore, "we love Him because He first loved us" (1 John 4:19).

Theological Explanation:

The melody "Agios" explains the reality of the unity of divinity with humanity in the person of our Lord Jesus Christ. The Holy Mighty Living God who is not subject to death is the very one who was born of the Virgin, crucified for us, rose from the dead, and ascended to heaven. It is not that Jesus Christ is two persons, one God and the other human. We cannot speak of two separate natures in the one person of our Lord Jesus Christ after the union. But He is the same one glorified with the Father and the Holy Spirit. He is the one who accepted humiliation and death through the cross, and we worship Him and glorify Him.

This awesome hymn is considered a profound response to the heresy of Nestorius, who taught that it is not permissible to say that God was crucified and died. According to Nestorius, the one crucified – in his view – was only a human. He also said that the Virgin did not give birth to an incarnate God but to a mere human, and God came upon Him at His baptism. This hymn came to calmly respond to this dangerous heresy. Indeed, God is the one born of the Virgin, who suffered, was crucified, died for us, and rose gloriously.

The Deacon Simon ben Kalil from the 12th century said, "Every time they say Agios, they make the sign of the cross, the sign of sanctification they received from the Only Begotten Son. For He is our powerful and living God, who was incarnated, died, and rose. Therefore, they conclude Agios by glorifying the Trinity, thanking the Father, the Son, and the Holy Spirit for the grace of eternal life, qualifying them to hear the Gospel they proclaim."

The Reading of the Gospel:

The Psalm:

The Psalm preceding the Gospel has a profound theological and contemplative weight, as it anticipates and points to the Lord Jesus Christ with the spirit of prophecy, similar to John the Baptist. So, when we hear the deacon chanting, "Psalm of David," it means "a psalm about David." And the word "David" here in Greek is in the genitive case so the expression is not "psalm by David" but "psalm about David."

David is the prophetic and code name for our Lord Jesus Christ:

"Afterward the children of Israel shall return and seek the Lord their God and David their king. They shall fear the Lord and His goodness in the latter days" (Hosea 3:5).

"I will save My flock, and they shall no longer be a prey; and I will judge between sheep and sheep. I will establish one shepherd over them, and he shall feed them—My servant David. He shall feed them and be their shepherd. And I, the Lord, will be their God, and My servant David a prince among them. I, the Lord, have spoken" (Ezekiel 34:22-24).

"David, my servant, shall be king over them, and they shall all have one shepherd." (Ezekiel 37:24).

"And my servant David shall be their prince forever." (Ezekiel 37:25).

"They shall serve the Lord their God and David their king, whom I will raise up for them." (Jeremiah 30:9).

It is quite clear that these prophets are not speaking of David the son of Jesse, as they came many generations after him. Instead, they speak in the spirit of prophecy about our new David, our Lord Jesus Christ. The word "David" in Hebrew is equivalent to the Arabic word "Wadood," meaning "beloved." It is a title for Christ. "To the praise of the glory of His grace, by which he made us accepted in the Beloved" (Ephesians 1:6). Thus, the preceding Psalm for the Gospel always speaks prophetically about our Lord Jesus Christ, emerging His presence to us in the church and comforting His people with the words of His life-giving grace. The Psalm also directs the reader's mind to the central theme of the church readings in its order of the Katameros.

The Gospel reading is the climax of the Divine Liturgy of the Catechumens and the peak of the sacred readings. Therefore, it is preceded by the prayer of the litany of the Gospel and the procession of the Gospel around the altar. Then the deacon calls out, "Stand up in the fear of God and listen to the Holy Gospel."

There are special hymns for the responses preceding the Psalm of the Gospel and the responses after the Gospel reading, tailored to the specific Gospel and the occasion being celebrated.

The procession of the priest and the deacon around the altar with the Gospel, the cross, and the incense signifies the proclamation of the Gospel and faith in the Cross throughout the world. During this procession, the priest secretly prays the prayer of Simeon the Elder when he carried the infant Christ in his arms, saying, "Lord, now You are letting Your servant depart in peace, According to Your word; For my eyes have seen Your salvation, Which You have prepared before the face of all peoples, A light to bring revelation to the Gentiles, And the glory of Your people Israel." (Luke 2:29-32). Meanwhile, the chanters chant some selected verses from the psalms after the Psalm is chanted in Coptic. This is called the "Psalms Procession" because it is recited during the procession of the Gospel around the altar, consisting of selected verses from the Psalms.

The Gospel reading in the church is a personal presence of the Lord Jesus Christ, we express it by the phrase "Blessed is He who comes in the name of the Lord" and with giving incense towards the

Gospel while the priest says, "Worship the Gospel of Jesus Christ." Therefore, the lights and candles are lit not only for illumination but also as a sign of joy for the Gospel and the presence of Christ, indicating the enlightenment we receive from the Gospel.

"Your word is a lamp to my feet and a light to my path." (Psalm 119:105).

"For the commandment is a lamp, and the law a light; reproofs of instruction are the way of life." (Proverbs 6:23).

"The law of the Lord is perfect, converting the soul; the testimony of the Lord is sure, making wise the simple. The statutes of the Lord are right, rejoicing the heart; the commandment of the Lord is pure, enlightening the eyes." (Psalm 19:7-8).

The deacon's call, "Stand up in the fear of God and listen…" signifies that everyone should stand still, not walk or speak, but focus only on hearing the word of God. If someone enters the church or passes by it during the Gospel reading, they should stand in place without movement until the reading is completed. It is very woeful for someone to cause any disturbance or movement that distracts the worshipers from listening to the gospel, and the warning applies: "Woe to that man by whom the offense comes!" (Matthew 18:7).

We have an excellent model of how to read the word of God with fear and respect during the return from captivity in the days of Nehemiah. The Holy Scripture describes a magnificent scene, "Now all the people gathered together as one man in the open square that was in front of the Water Gate; and they told Ezra the scribe to bring the Book of the Law of Moses, which the Lord had commanded Israel. So Ezra the priest brought the Law before the assembly of men and women and all who could hear with understanding on the first day of the seventh month. Then he read from it in the open square that was in front of the Water Gate from morning until midday, before the men and women and those who could understand; and the ears of all the people were attentive to the Book of the Law. So Ezra the scribe stood on a platform of wood which they had made for the purpose; and beside him, at his right hand, stood Mattithiah, Shema, Anaiah, Urijah, Hilkiah, and Maaseiah; and at his left hand

Pedaiah, Mishael, Malchijah, Hashum, Hashbadana, Zechariah, and Meshullam. And Ezra opened the book in the sight of all the people, for he was standing above all the people; and when he opened it, all the people stood up. And Ezra blessed the Lord, the great God. Then all the people answered, "Amen, Amen!" while lifting up their hands. And they bowed their heads and worshiped the Lord with their faces to the ground. Also Jeshua, Bani, Sherebiah, Jamin, Akkub, Shabbethai, Hodijah, Maaseiah, Kelita, Azariah, Jozabad, Hanan, Pelaiah, and the Levites, helped the people to understand the Law; and the people stood in their place. So they read distinctly from the book, in the Law of God; and they gave the sense, and helped them to understand the reading. And Nehemiah, who was the governor, Ezra the priest and scribe, and the Levites who taught the people said to all the people, "This day is holy to the Lord your God; do not mourn nor weep." For all the people wept, when they heard the words of the Law. Then he said to them, "Go your way, eat the fat, drink the sweet, and send portions to those for whom nothing is prepared; for this day is holy to our Lord. Do not sorrow, for the joy of the Lord is your strength." So the Levites quieted all the people, saying, "Be still, for the day is holy; do not be grieved." And all the people went their way to eat and drink, to send portions and rejoice greatly, because they understood the words that were declared to them." (Nehemiah 8:1-12).

The Gospel reader, whether a priest or a deacon, kisses the Gospel before and after its reading. Kissing before the reading indicates readiness to listen and act upon the Gospel, and kissing after the reading signifies belief and submission. In the past, the entire congregation used to approach to kiss the Gospel after its reading.[1]

All these liturgical practices affirm the church's faith in the special presence of the Lord Jesus Christ during the reading of the Holy Gospel.

---

1 Note: As an exception only in Pasha week starting Wednesday eve till the feast of resurrection, the reader doesn't kiss the Gospel, the cross, the veils, or the priests' hands in condemnation of Judas' kiss.

CHAPTER 9

The Litanies

"The term Litanies (ouashy) is of Coptic origin, derived from the plural of 'Oushiya,' meaning prayers. In the Divine Liturgy and all our liturgical prayers, we offer these litanies, presenting our needs to our Almighty God, believing that we will receive what we have asked for.

- "Be anxious for nothing, but in everything by prayer and supplication, with thanksgiving, let your requests be made known to God" (Philippians 4:6).

- "Praying always with all prayer and supplication in the Spirit, being watchful to this end with all perseverance and supplication for all the saints" (Ephesians 6:18).

- "Let us, therefore, come boldly to the throne of grace, that we may obtain mercy and find grace to help in time of need" (Hebrews 4:16).

- "And whatever we ask we receive from Him because we keep His commandments and do those things that are pleasing in His sight" (1 John 3:22).

- "Ask, and it will be given to you; seek, and you will find; knock, and it will be opened to you" (Matthew 7:7).

- "Until now you have asked nothing in My name. Ask, and you will receive, that your joy may be full" (John 16:24).

Our loving and merciful God delights in our requests, responding with His love and providence for our lives.

The prayers of the litanies are very ancient. Saint Justin Martyr from the second century AD said, 'We pray fervently together for our souls, for the baptized, and for all others everywhere, that we may worthy of knowing the truth. For by doing good works and keeping the commandments, we may obtain eternal salvation.'

The power of the litanies, and their ability to ascend before the throne of God to be action, lies in the participation of the entire Church. The Church as a whole prays and pleads. Here, the priest is not a substitute for the people in prayer; rather, he may pray on behalf of the people in some prayers, but all the people participate, ensuring that the prayer of the priest is ultimately the prayer of the entire Church. Here, the prayers reach their peak strength, and the Church is exalted in its entirety.

The responsibility of praying for the people does not rest solely on the priests; the people are also responsible for praying for their priests. The prayers of both groups for each other complete the meaning of the Church as living members in one body, the body of Christ.

The Ouashy used in the Church consists of about eighteen prayers, which I will list and then discuss in detail:

1. Litany of the Departed: For those who preceded us into paradise.

2. Litany of the Sick: Prayed for our fathers and brethren who are sick with every sickness.

3. Litany of Travelers: Prayed for our fathers and brethren who are travelling

4. Litany of Oblations: There are two litanies of oblation: one prayed during matins, which is long, and one prayed in the liturgy which is short.

5. Litany of the Gospel: Prayed for the hearing of the Gospel and keeping the commandments.

6. Litany of Peace: That is, the peace of the Church, and there are

The Litanies

two; great and short.

7. Litany of the Fathers: For the Pope and bishops, and there are two; great and short.

8. Litany of Assemblies: Prayed for the success of our spiritual, liturgical, and educational meetings.

9. Litany of the Place: Prayed for the salvation of the world and our city, in the raising of the evening incense

10. Litany of Air, Fruits, and Water: According to the season.

11. Litany of Mercy: "Remember, O Lord, to have mercy on us all" said during the liturgy.

12. Litany of the Hegumens, Priests, and Deacons: And all who are in virginity, all the people, and the servants.

13. Litany of the President (Leaders): Rulers, and ministers.

14. Litany of Government Employees: Those in the palaces and all soldiers.

15. Litany of the Captives: Whether in wars, prisons, or captives due to sin.

16. Litany of those who are standing in this place and the rest of the Orthodox: So that we do not forget anyone.

17. Litany of the Catechumens: Those who believed in Christ but have not received baptism yet.

18. Litany of the Distressed: For God to relieve their distress.

Our glorious Church, when standing before God, forgets no one and nothing. We pray for everyone, and even during the priests' absolution following the midnight watches, the priest prays for those who have no one to remember them, namely the forgotten, marginalized, scorned, and absent. Truly, everyone is important before God.

As the Holy Scriptures say, "Pray for one another, that you may be healed. The effective, fervent prayer of a righteous man avails much" (James 5:16). This prayer expresses our concern for one another, "Be of the same mind toward one another" (Romans 12:16). We are all members of one body, and it is necessary for each to care for the other because of this sacred membership in the body of Christ.

Our Church here resembles the four men who carried the paralytic to the Lord Jesus. "When Jesus saw their faith, He said to the paralytic, "Son, your sins are forgiven you"" (Mark 2:5). Although God knows our needs before we ask Him, He loves for us to talk to Him about these matters, declaring our love for fellowship. "For your Father knows the things you have need of before you ask Him" (Matthew 6:8)".

The Litany of the Departed

The Church prays the litany of the departed daily during the raising of evening incense, as well as, the raising of morning incense on Saturdays.

But why do we pray for the departed? Hasn't their eternal state been settled on the day they departed from the body? Do the prayers of the Church for them change their state or benefit them in any way? And if it doesn't benefit them, why do we pray for them in funerals, commemorations, and the litany of the departed?

The answer is that our prayers for the departed express our faith in several points:

(1) Faith that they are still alive:

"I am the God of Abraham, the God of Isaac, and the God of Jacob? God is not the God of the dead, but of the living" (Matthew 22:32).

(2) Faith that they are still members of the body of Christ, of which we are also members:

"For as we have many members in one body, but all the members do not have the same function (Romans 12:5).

"for we are members of one another " (Ephesians 4:35).

And the members feel for each other for "if one member suffers, all the members suffer with it; or if one member is honored, all the members rejoice with it" (1 Corinthians 26:12).

Active members in one body are required to pray for each other.

"I beg you, brethren, through the Lord Jesus Christ, and through the love of the Spirit, that you strive together with me in prayers to God for me" (Romans 15:30).

"Do not cease to give thanks for you, making mention of you in my prayers." (Ephesians 1:16).

"Brethren, pray for us." (1 Thessalonians 5:25).

"I exhort first of all that supplications, prayers, intercessions, and giving of thanks be made for all men" (1 Timothy 2:1).

"Confess your trespasses to one another, and pray for one another, that you may be healed. The effective, fervent prayer of a righteous man avails much" (James 5:16).

(3) Faith in the resurrection of the dead:

That we will meet together on the last day, "the hour is coming, and now is, when the dead will hear the voice of the Son of God; and those who hear will live. For as the Father has life in Himself, so He has granted the Son to have life in Himself, and has given Him authority to execute judgment." (John 5:28-29).

"Therefore my heart rejoiced, and my tongue was glad; Moreover my flesh also will rest in hope (Acts 2:26).

(4) Faith in the connection between heaven and earth:

"Giving thanks to the Father who has qualified us to be partakers of the inheritance of the saints in the light" (Colossians 1:12).

"The beggar died, and was carried by the angels to Abraham's bosom. The rich man also died and was buried." (Luke 16:22).

We believe that we will dwell in the bosom of the saints, so how can we not pray for them, and they for us, now?

(5) Consolation for the living:

Praying for the departed consoles their living relatives and makes them feel the church's companionship with them and participation in their painful feelings, "Rejoice with those who rejoice, weep with them that weep" (Romans 12:15). Therefore, the prayers of the funeral begin with the litany of the sick, considering that the relatives of the deceased are in a state of mental exhaustion and need prayers, "The Lord grant mercy to the household of Onesiphorus, for he often refreshed me, and was not ashamed of my chain" (2 Timothy 16:1).

(6) Honor and respect for the body:

"Do you not know that your bodies are members of Christ?" (1 Corinthians 6:15). We believe that the soul of the departed has gone to the places of rest, and the embalmed body before us is also sacred because:

- It was baptized with the Holy Trinity:

"For as many of you as were baptized into Christ have put on Christ." (Galatians 3:27).

- It was anointed with holy Myron and became a dwelling place for the Holy Spirit:

"Do you not know that you are God's temple and that God's Spirit dwells in you?" (1 Corinthians 3:16).

- It united many times with the Body and Blood of the Lord in the mystery of the Holy Communion:

"He who eats My flesh and drinks My blood abides in Me, and I in him" (John 6:56).

- It toiled in the service of Christ, the Church, people, and ascetic life:

"But I discipline my body and bring it into subjection, lest, when I have preached to others, I myself should become disqualified" (1 Corinthians 9:27).

"For I bear in my body the marks of the Lord Jesus." (Galatians 6:17).

(7) Seeking mercy for the departed:

As Saint Paul sought mercy for Onesiphorus, saying, "The Lord grant to him that he may find mercy from the Lord in that Day" (2 Timothy 1:18), where "that Day" means the day of judgment.

(8) Praying for the departed is the completion of the repentance of the repentant departed:

The repentant departed is a person who lived a holy life on earth but was not without weaknesses and falls. Like other believers, he presented daily or even momentary repentance. Upon his departure from the earth, the angels take him to the dwelling of the righteous in the paradise.

But Satan continues to complain against him even after entering paradise, citing forgotten old sins or mistakes, considering them sufficient reason to possess his soul. Satan will continue to complain against humans until the last day when the cry of victory comes from heaven, saying, "Now salvation, and strength, and the kingdom of our God, and the power of His Christ have come, for the accuser of our brethren, who accused them before our God day and night, has been cast down" (Revelation 12:10).

So, when the church prays for the departed, their repentance becomes completes, closing the door on Satan and silencing him. That's why we say in the litany of the departed, "even if any negligence or heedlessness have overtaken them as men, since they were clothed in flesh and dwelt in this world, O God, as the Good One and Lover of Mankind, graciously accord, O lord to repose and forgive them". The capacity for the forgiveness of unintentional transgressions or oversights is found in the verse, "anyone who speaks a word against the Son of Man, it will be forgiven him; but whoever speaks against the Holy Spirit, it will not be forgiven him either in this age or in the age to come" (Matthew 12:32).

Of course, only the saints, who have completed their struggle on earth and entered paradise, benefit from these prayers, but Satan still complains against them.

As for the evildoers, unbelievers, and those immersed in sin and evil, millions of prayers for them are of no avail, as their hope has been lost. Therefore, the church does not pray for the unbelieving dead or those who have deviated from the straight path, and it does not pray for those who have committed suicide, or those who died in their sin, whether caught or killed, because they committed a grave sin.

Regarding prayers for the departed, Saint Cyril of Jerusalem (4th century AD) explains, "And I wish to persuade you by an illustration. For I know that many say, what is a soul profited, which departs from this world either with sins, or without sins, if it be commemorated in the prayer? For if a king were to banish certain who had given him offense, and then those who belong to them should weave a crown and offer it to him on behalf of those under punishment, would he not grant a remission of their penalties? In the same way we, when we offer to Him our supplications for those who have fallen asleep, though they be sinners, weave no crown, but offer up Christ sacrificed for our sins, propitiating our merciful God for them as well as for ourselves"[1]

(9) Alerting the minds of believers to the beauty of eternity:

In the prayers for the departed, we say:

- "May they, O Lord, find repose in the bosom of our holy fathers, Abraham, Isaac, and Jacob."

"So it was that the beggar died, and was carried by the angels to Abraham's bosom. The rich man also died and was buried." (Luke 16:22).

- "They shall obtain joy and gladness, and sorrow and sighing shall flee away" (Isaiah 35:10).

"And I heard a loud voice from heaven saying, "Behold, the tabernacle of God is with men, and He will dwell with them, and they shall be His people. God Himself will be with them and be their God. And God will wipe away every tear from their eyes; there shall be no

---

[1] Catechetical Lecture 23

more death, nor sorrow, nor crying. There shall be no more pain, for the former things have passed away" (Revelation 21:3-4).

"Grant them the riches of your promises. What no eye has seen, nor ear heard, nor the heart of man conceived, what you, O God, have prepared for those who love your holy name." "But as it is written: 'Eye has not seen, nor ear heard, Nor have entered into the heart of man, The things which God has prepared for those who love Him'" (1 Corinthians 2:9).

The Diptych

After the Commemoration in the liturgy, the priest says inaudibly: "Remember, O Lord, all those who have fallen asleep and reposed in the in the priesthood, and in all the orders of the laity. Graciously, O Lord, repose all their souls in the bosom of our holy fathers Abraham, Isaac and Jacob. Sustain them in green pastures beside still waters in the paradise of joy, the place out of which grief, sorry, and groaning have fled away in the light of Your saints".

If there is a commemoration for one of the departed, the following is read as part of the diptych: "Those, O Lord, and everyone whose names we have mentioned, and those we have not mentioned, those whom each of us has in mind and those who are not in mind, who have fallen asleep and reposed in the faith of Christ ".

Then, the names of the departed are mentioned individually, and incense is placed in the censer as a sign that these prayers ascend to heaven for them. Then, the beautiful and profound prayer is said secretly: "O Holy Trinity, have mercy on us. O Holy Trinity, forgive us our sins. O Holy Trinity, accept this offering from us, weak sinners. Remember, O Lord, our fathers and brethren who have fallen asleep from among your people and all those whom we have been asked to remember in our prayers, especially Your servant (name) whom we have offered these gifts for today. May it be a good remembrance for him on Your holy altar. Forgive his sins and transgressions through the intercessions of the holy and pure Mother of God St Mary and all Your saints, for You are the one who befits glory, O Father, Son, and Holy Spirit, now and at all times."

The priest raises his hands upward and prays after the diptych: "Those, O Lord, whose souls You have taken, repose them in the Paradise of joy, in the region of the living for ever, in the heavenly Jerusalem, in that place". Here, the church calls the paradise of joy (the region of the living) as if we are on earth in the region of the dead. As for those whom people consider dead, they are resting in the paradise of joy forever in the heavenly Jerusalem.

"And we, too, who are sojourners in this place, keep us in Your faith, and grant us Your peace unto the end". We are strangers in this world (this place), so Saint Peter warns us: "conduct yourselves throughout the time of your stay here in fear" (1 Peter 1:17). We pray with the psalmist, "I am a stranger on earth; do not hide Your commands from me" (Psalm 119:19). All we ask during this pilgrimage on earth is that God keeps us on the straight and narrow path of the Christian faith until the very end and grants us to know the way to the kingdom;. "Lead us throughout the way into Your kingdom".

Lord Jesus, I thank you for this beautiful church that delivered to us the mystery of faith and taught us how to communicate with You and what to ask of You. You entrusted us the mystery of Your will when You taught us, "Seek first the kingdom of God and His righteousness" (Matthew 6:33). O Good God, I implore You not to deprive me of Your kingdom, no matter my sins, ignorance, weaknesses, or shortcomings. For You are a merciful God, lover of mankind, benevolent, desiring the salvation of all.

Why do we pray for the departed at the evening hour?

It is fitting to mention the departed at the evening hour, as the evening reminds us of the end of the day and its activities, and returning to the eternal home rest.

"For man goes to his eternal home" (Ecclesiastes 12:5).

"But the saints of the Most High shall receive the kingdom, and possess the kingdom forever, even forever and ever" (Daniel 7:18).

"And many of those who sleep in the dust of the earth shall awake, Some to everlasting life, Some to shame and everlasting contempt" (Daniel 12:2).

The sorrows associated with death befit the evening time, 'Weeping may endure for a night, but joy comes in the morning' (Psalm 30:5).

Similarly, we pray the same litany of the departd during the raising of morning incense on Saturday because Saturday symbolises the day of repose (the end of the week) at the end of life. That is why our Lord Jesus Christ chose the day of His repose in the tomb to be the entire Saturday, and then the day of resurrection to be the dawn of Sunday, the new day of the new week.

Litany of the sick

As for the remaining days, we pray for the sick and the travellers during matins. This is because the dawn of the day symbolizes hope and optimism. The sunrise every day means that God gives us a new opportunity for repentance, life, productivity, and improving our conditions. Thus, with the new sunrise, we lift our prayers up for our brethren who are sick and travelling so that optimism and hope are renewed in them through healing and their safe return to their homes.

In the Litany of the Sick, the Church expresses with profound spiritual beauty the spirit of fellowship and empathy. We pray for our fathers and our brethren the sick, with all forms of illnesses, that God my remove from their hearts the spirit of weakness, delirium and sickness; "the spirit of sicknesses, chase away".

It is of the nature of the Church that we are all together, "Now all who believed were together, and had all things in common" (Acts 2:44). The sign of our membership in the one body is feeling for one another, "And if one member suffers, all the members suffer with it" (1 Corinthians 12:26).

The Church expresses these sentiments through praying for the sick. No doubt, illness hinders a person from fellowship with the

Church in terms of fasting, energetic prayer, gathering in the Holy Church for Eucharist or Liturgy, preaching and teaching. Therefore, when one of the members is absent due to illness, the church gathers around them to pray by performing the sacrament of the Unction of the Sick. We also pray for them in the litany of the sick every day during matins; "Remember, O Lord, the sick among Your people". We also pray for those with chronic diseases: "Those who have long lain in maladies, raise up and comfort".

Moreover, we pray for those tormented by unclean spirits, "set them all free... and have mercy upon them". Likewise those tormented psychologically due to imprisonment, exile, captivity, being held in bitter bondage (the bondage of Satan, people or ego). For the church rejoices in the freedom, comfort, joy, and stability of people, and prays for everyone, not forgetting anyone.

The church here in its prayers distinguishes between physical diseases resulting from infection or weakness in bodily organs, other mental health illnesses due to external factors or hormonal or biochemical imbalances, and thirdly, malady resulting from unclean spirits. Not all psychiatric conditions are interpreted as unclean spirits, just as psychiatric medicine cannot ignore cases of unclean spirits that need prayers and special grace to expel the demons. All of these need the prayers of the church for them without neglecting the role of the doctor and medical treatment.

Our Lord Jesus Christ, to whom is the glory, endorse the role of the doctor in treatment when He said, "Those who are well have no need of a physician, but those who are sick" (Matthew 9:12).

The Book of Sirach speaks extensively about the role of the physician in healing:

1. "Honour physicians for their services, for the Lord created them;" (Sirach 38:1).

2. "The skill of physicians makes them distinguished, and in the presence of the great they are admired." (Sirach 38:3).

3. "Then give the physician his place, for the Lord created him; do not let him leave you, for you need him" (Sirach 38:12).

4. "There may come a time when recovery lies in the hands of physicians" (Sirach 38:13).

The litany of the sick and the Unction of the Sick do not negate the role of the physician and medical treatment. However, it is also not appropriate to rely solely on human efforts, forgetting our Almighty God, who grants healing.

In the same vein, we recall the example of King Asa, "And in the thirty-ninth year of his reign, Asa became diseased in his feet, and his malady was severe; yet in his disease he did not seek the LORD, but the physicians" (2 Chronicles 16:12). Therefore, we turn to physicians, praying to God for healing, saying, "You have visited them with mercies and compassions, health them… For You are He who loosens the bound and lifts up the fallen; the hope of those who have no hope and the help of those who have no helper; the comfort of the fainthearted (discouraged souls feeling small due to prolonged or incurable illness); the harbour of those in the storm (all of life's storms- its hardships, pains, distress and people's rejection of us). All souls that are distressed or bound (either financially, spiritually or emotionally), grant them mercy, O Lord; grant them rest… refreshment.. grace… help… salvation (from its severity)… forgiveness of their sins and their iniquities"

1. St. James explicitly connects healing and forgiveness when he says, "Is anyone among you sick? Let him call for the elders of the church, and let them pray over him, anointing him with oil in the name of the Lord. And the prayer of faith will save the one who is sick, and the Lord will raise him up. And if he has committed sins, he will be forgiven" (James 5:14-15).

2. Similarly, Jesus links forgiveness and healing in the healing of the paralysed man let down from the roof, saying, " Then behold, they brought to Him a paralytic lying on a bed. When Jesus saw their faith, He said to the paralytic, "Son, be of good cheer; your sins are forgiven you" (Matthew 9:2).

3. Likewise, in the healing of the sick at the pool of Bethesda, Jesus said to him "See, you have been made well. Sin no more, lest a worse thing come upon you" (John 5:14).

While sin may be a cause of illness, not every illness is caused by sin. However, human nature, in general, has been subjected to sickness, weakness, and corruption due to the entrance of sin since Adam. Hence, there is a strong connection between sin and illness.

This prompts us that during our times of illness, we should take a moment to repent and review the course of our lives. However, it is not required of us to condemn the sick, expecting that they are being punished because they have sinned. Therefore, at the end of the prayers, the priest prays and says, "As for us, too, O Lord, the sicknesses of our souls, heal; and also those of our bodies, cure. O You, the true physician of our souls and bodies, the Bishop of all flesh, visit us with Your salvation."

Prayers for Travelers

After the prayers for the sick, there are prayers for our fathers and brethren who are traveling everywhere, as if the Church wants to emphasize the lesson of caring for others, especially those absent from us in body. It is the spirit of fellowship that should dominate our church life.

1. " Let brotherly love continue. Do not forget to entertain strangers, for by so doing some have unwittingly entertained angels. Remember the prisoners as if chained with them—those who are mistreated—since you yourselves are in the body also." (Hebrews 13:1-3).

2. "Be of the same mind toward one another. Do not set your mind on high things, but associate with the humble. Do not be wise in your own opinion" (Romans 12:16).

The Bible specifically teaches us to care for the traveller, the guest, and the stranger; "distributing to the needs of the saints, given to hospitality" (Romans 12:13)

Further, hospitality towards guests and strangers was one of the traits of Job the righteous. "But no sojourner had to lodge in the street, for I have opened my doors to the traveller" (Job 31:32).

In fact, there are many commandments regarding the good treatment of guests, strangers and travellers:

"And if a stranger dwells with you in your land, you shall not mistreat him" (Leviticus 19:33).

"You shall neither mistreat a stranger nor oppress him, for you were strangers in the land of Egypt" (Exodus 22:21).

Our fathers always felt that they were strangers and travellers on earth:

"I am a foreigner and a visitor among you" (Genesis 23:4).

"Hear my prayer, O Lord, And give ear to my cry; Do not be silent at my tears; For I am a stranger with You, A sojourner, as all my fathers were" (Psalm 39:12).

"I am a stranger in the earth; Do not hide Your commandments from me" (Psalm 119:19).

Jesus encouraged hospitality towards strangers when He considered that whoever receives a stranger is as if he welcomed the Lord Himself, "I was a stranger and you took Me in" (Matthew 25:35). And our teacher, the Apostle Peter, reminded us that showing hospitality should be done joyfully, "Be hospitable to one another without grumbling" (1 Peter 4:9).

The Church expresses its service towards guests, travellers, and strangers through praying for them, and even for those who even just contemplate travel (think about it and plan it in their consciences). We pray that God facilitates their journeys altogether and prevents accidents, disasters, and breakdowns, whether traveling by sea, rivers, lakes, air, roads, or any other form of travel.

We pray for travellers of all kinds and modes of transportation, as well as for everyone in every place, whether we know them or not, whether they share our faith or not.

It is a prayer for all of humanity who are on their daily journeys for livelihood, work, leisure, and visits. We pray for God to bring them back to a "quiet harbor, the harbor of salvation."

How beautiful it is for a person to find tranquillity and deliverance after a long journey. It is a symbol of the final harbor that the soul peacefully reaches after a long journey of struggle with the waves, currents, storms, and dangers of life on earth. It is the long-awaited day when the soul anchors in the embrace of the saints and in the presence of the Lord Himself.

The Church prays not only for a safe and sound arrival but also that God accompanies them in take-off (the beginning of the journey) and during the journey (throughout the way). May God send them an angel to guard them from the evils of the road, just as the chief of the angels, Raphael, was sent to accompany Tobias the son on his long journey.

Then, we pray for a peaceful return, "Bring them back to their own, rejoicing with joy and safe in security" for the success of the travel and their safe and healthy return. We pray for God to share us in every good deed, for God shares our travels and journeys if they are for good and not for sin or evil.

We conclude the prayers by praying for ourselves, the strangers in this world, saying: "As for us, too, O Lord, keep our sojourn in this life without harm, without storm and undisturbed to the end".

For we are also travellers to our heavenly homeland, desiring to return to it safely, triumphant, with a healthy body, soul, and spirit, to enjoy the company of the saints:

"Having a desire to depart and be with Christ, which is far better" (Philippians 1:23).

For man, "born of woman, is of few days and full of trouble. He comes forth like a flower and fades away; he flees like a shadow and does not continue" (Job 14:1-2).

And at the end of his journey "like a hired man, he finishes his day" (Job 14:6).

The Litany of the Oblations:

The Church prays the litany of oblations (the long one) during the raising of the morning incense after the litany for the sick, and instead of the prayers for travellers. This happens on days when the liturgy is immediately after matins, which are the days without abstinent fasting (feasts, Sundays, and non-fasting days).

If there is abstinent fasting, the liturgy is supposed to be later, so the Church prays for the travellers after the litany of the sick in the raising of the morning incense, and the litany of the oblations is postponed and prayed inaudibly during the prayer of Incense for the Praxis

The word "korban" (oblation) means "gift," so when we offer our oblations (karabeen) to God, we present Him with our gifts. As we believe that all things are gifts from God to us, we say to Him, "We offer You Your gifts from what is Yours" as David the prophet said, "For all things come from You, and of Your own we have given You" (1 Chronicles 29:14).

"O Lord our God, all this abundance that we have prepared to build You a house for Your holy name is from Your hand, and is all Your own" (1 Chronicles 29:16).

The oblations we present to God are not only bread and wine, but everything offered in the church. This is evident in the deacon's response in the Litany of Oblations "Pray for those who provide for the sacrifices, offerings, first fruits (the first product or production), oil (for the lamps), incense, coverings, reading books, and altar vessels...".

We also offer time, effort, care, money, and service, all for the glory of God and the edification of the church. Presenting these gifts expresses our faith that all things are from God and are also for Him.

For example, offering the tithes means that I return to God everything He has given me in salary, revenue, or product, then receive from His divine hand nine-tenths as a reward. What is in my hands becomes a gift given to me by God, not from people, and this is the reason for the blessing.

""Bring all the tithes into the storehouse, that there may be food in My house, and try Me now in this," says the Lord of hosts, "If I will not open for you the windows of heaven and pour out for you such blessing that there will not be room enough to receive it"" (Malachi 3:10).

Furthermore, vows, first fruits, and optional offerings (beyond the required) are also included in the scope of offerings. Therefore, the Church prays for those who have toiled and presented these offerings.

There are two litanies for the oblations; great and short (in terms of the length of the prayers):

The short litany is prayed in the Liturgy of St Basil Liturgy before the Commemoration, and likewise at the beginning of the liturgy with the offering of the lamb. The priest says, "Remember, O Lord, those who have brought to You these gifts (the givers themselves), those on whose behalf they have been brought (whether the departed, the sick, the distressed, or those who have asked us to offer on their behalf), and those by whom they have been brought (the priest, deacon, and the congregation in attendance). Give them all the heavenly reward (eternal bliss).

God has promised that the reward of service will not be lost, even if it is just a cup of cold water, "And whoever gives one of these little ones only a cup of cold water in the name of a disciple, assuredly, I say to you, he shall by no means lose his reward" (Matthew 10:42).

There is a sincere divine promise of eternal happiness for the pure servants of Christ:

"If anyone serves Me, let him follow Me; and where I am, there My servant will be also. If anyone serves Me, him My Father will honor" (John 12:26).

As for the great litany of oblations, it is prayed in the matins or before the Praxis. The priest says in it, "Receive them upon Your holy, rational altar in heaven as a sweet savour of incense

"Christ also has loved us and given Himself for us, an offering and a sacrifice to God for a sweet-smelling aroma" (Ephesians 5:2).

This incense rises to Your greatness in the heavens through the service of Your angels and archangels, "A thousands, thousands ministered to Him; Ten thousand times ten thousand stood before Him" (Daniel 7:10). Just as You accepted the offerings of Abel the righteous, "Abel also brought of the firstborn of his flock and of their fat. And the Lord respected Abel and his offering" (Genesis 4:4), and the sacrifice of our father Abraham (Genesis 22), and the widow's two mites, "Then one poor widow came and threw in two mites, which make a quadrans. So He called His disciples to Himself and said to them, 'Assuredly, I say to you that this poor widow has put in more than all those who have given to the treasury; for they all put in out of their abundance, but she out of her poverty put in all that she had, her whole livelihood'" (Mark 12:42-44).

Likewise, "receive the thank offerings of Your servants- those in abundance or those in scarcity, hidden or manifest- those who desire to offer to You but have none, and those who have offered these gift to You this very day. Give them the incorruptible instead of the corruptible, the heavenly instead of the earthly, and the eternal instead of the temporal. Their houses and their stores fill them with every good thing. Surround them, O Lord, by the power of Your holy angels and archangels. As they have remembered Your holy name on earth, remember them also, O Lord, in Your kingdom, and in this age, too, leave them not behind".

This litany is prayed in an extremely beautiful melody that carries the meaning of supplication, insistence, and gentle request to God, so that He rewards everyone whose heart urges him to give. Thus, the church is filled with goods which are distributed to the poor, contributing to the continuation of service in the church, and the livelihood of the servants. As it is said, "Do you not know that those who minister the holy things eat of the things of the temple, and those who serve at the altar partake of the offerings of the altar?" (1 Corinthians 9:13).

The Litany of the Gospel

The Holy Bible holds a very high status in the Orthodox Church, as it is God's revealed thought for the salvation of humans. The Orthodox Church encourages us to read the Holy Bible, whether individually or collectively, at home or in the church. However, in interpretation, we must adhere to the thought of the Fathers so that the interpretation does not deviate from the right framework.

Reading the Gospel in the liturgy has a very special honour. Therefore, it is preceded by a prayer called "The Litany of the Gospel," which is prayed after the hymn "Agios" in the liturgy and after "Efnooti Nai Nan" in the Raising of Evening and Morning incense

This litany describes, in a way, the secret presence of the Lord Christ in the church through the reading of the Gospel. The priest says, "O Master, Lord Jesus Christ our God, who said to His saintly, honoured disciples and holy apostles, "Many prophets and righteous men have desired to see the things which you see, and have not seen them, and to hear the things which you hear, and have not heard them. But as for you, blessed are your eyes, for they see, and your ears, for they hear". May we be worthy to hear and to act according to Your Holy Gospels, through the prayers of Your saints". Therefore, the Lord Christ, who was present among His saintly disciples, blessed their eyes and ears because they saw and heard Him. Likewise, He, Himself, blesses our eyes and ears now, as He is also present in the midst of His Church, teaching us with His pure mouth as He did with the apostles and every generation. He is present everywhere and at all times, saying, "fFor where two or three are gathered together in My name, I am there in the midst of them" (Matthew 18:20). As an expression of the presence of Christ, especially during the reading of the Gospel, the deacon proclaims, saying, "Stand in the fear of God and listen to the Holy Gospel, a passage from the Gospel according to Saint [name]." Then he says, "Blessed is He who comes in the name of the Lord."

The priest goes around the altar, and in front of him the deacon holding the Bishara (Gospels). He says secretly, "Lord, now you are letting Your servant depart in peace, according to Your word; for my eyes have seen Your salvation which you have prepared before the face of all peoples, a light to bring revelation to the Gentiles and the glory to Your people Israel" (Luke 2:29-32).

These are the same words uttered by the venerable elder Simeon, when he carried the infant (40 days old) Lord in his arms when He presented to the temple with His mother to offer the purification offering.

The priest also censes toward the Gospel as if censing the Lord Himself, praying inaudibly during the reading of the Gospel of the Divine Liturgy. This includes a set of litanies asking the Lord Christ our God, during His holy presence in the Church, to teach us through the Holy Gospel. These litanies include litanies for thhe sick, travellers, the departed, those offering gifts, the distressed, captives, the air, waters, plants, the catechumens… etc.

The mangaleya/analogion, which carries the Holy Gospel, is placed in an elevated spot to serve as a reminder of the Lord Jesus Christ, who "seeing the multitudes, He went up on a mountain, and when He was seated, His disciples came to Him. Then He opened His mouth and taught them…" (Matthew 5:1-2). It is fitting that the sublime teaching of the Lord is delivered from a high mountain.

By standing during the Gospel reading, the congregation expresses their respect for the presence of the Lord in the reading. It also signifies their readiness to implement and act upon what the Spirit speaks to the churches.

The act of standing also symbolizes the spiritual condition we should be in – standing victorious with Christ and ready for every good work.

The psalm read before the Gospel is always a prophecy about the Lord Jesus Christ, and is a guide to the main point of focus of the Gospel reading. It directs the reader, interpreter, and all who seek to benefit from the day's readings. We should follow along with the sacred readings with reverence, humility, tranquillity, attentive ears, and prepared hearts.

The reader should ensure clarity in the reading, with clear enunciation, avoiding the distortion of the clarity of the reading by the melody. The goal is for people to hear the voice of God, not the melody or the beauty of the reader's voice. Melodizing the Gospel reading aims to enhance concentration, not the other way around.

The Great Litanies

After the Veil Prayer[2] , the priest enters the sanctuary and prays the Great Litanies at the altar. These litanies are called "Great" due to the length of the prayers. There are also the shorter variations of these litanies with abbreviated prayers.

The Great Litanies are:

1. The Litany of Peace: Praying for the peace of the Church and the world.

2. The Litany of the Fathers: Praying for the Pope, bishops, clergy, and all the people.

3. The Litany of the Assemblies: Praying for spiritual gatherings to be blessed by God.

These litanies carry beautiful meanings in their prayers.

Firstly, the Litany of Peace:

In this litany, the priest says, "Remember, O Lord, the peace of Your one, holy, catholic, and apostolic Church... this which exists from one end of the world to the other, all peoples and all flocks, bless."

The Church prays for all peoples and churches, and while she takes pride in her Orthodoxy, she prays for all. This illustrates the principle that the Church is an assembly but is subdivided into peoples and flocks. The head of each flock is a bishop, and all collectively submit to the great Shepherd of Shepherds, the Lord Christ, who is represented by our fathers the Patriarchs.

In this litany, we pray for "the king (leader), the armies, the rulers,

---

[2] A deep prayer prayed by the priest in front of the entrance of the altar after the gospel is read.

the counsellors, the multitudes, our neighbours, our coming in and our going out", asking on their behalf for the Lord "to adorn them with all peace". The Church prays for the state and leaders for their peace and justice.

Interestingly, in eras of persecution, emperors and kings used to persecute the Church. Nevertheless, bishops, priests, and the people would stand, praying with all their hearts for the emperor or king, not for the end of the waves of persecution but for their peace, justice, and well-being. The Church teaches us to submit to authorities, even if they are against the Church. We obey them but in the Lord. Praying for leaders is a biblical command, as our teacher, the Apostle Paul, instructed us, saying, "Let every soul be subject to the governing authorities, for there is no authority except from God, and the authorities that exist are appointed by God" (Romans 13:1). This is because in their peace lies our peace, and stability in political matters of the nation leads to the peace and benefit of the Church.

- "Therefore, I exhort first of all that supplications, prayers, intercessions, and giving of thanks be made for all men, for kings and all who are in authority, that we may lead a quiet and peaceable life in all godliness and reverence" (1 Timothy 2:1-2).

- "And seek the peace of the city where I have caused you to be carried away captive, and pray to the Lord for it; for in its peace, you will have peace" (Jeremiah 29:7).

The priest continues saying, "O King of peace, grant us Your peace, for You have given us all things. Acquire us to Yourself, O god our Saviour, for we know none other but You. Your holy name we utter. May our souls live by Your Holy Spirit, and let not the death of sins have dominion over us, we Your servants, nor over all Your people".

You O God, gave us everything, that is why we ask you to also give us total peace which St Paul described as, "The peace of God which is beyond all understanding, guard your hearts and minds in Christ Jesus" (Philippians 4:7).

"Acquire us to Yourself, O God our Saviour"... Take us to be truly

Yours, so that we may become Your custody and share on this Earth which has drifted away from You and has become the share of the devil and evil. The devil has become the ruler of this world. He is a forceful captor, an imposter, a liar and the father of all liars. But we, Your people, are Yours, as for the evildoers, may they be the subject of this canticle, "Fear and dread will fall on them; by the greatness of Your arm they will be as still as a stone, till Your people pass over, O Lord, till the people pass over whom You have purchased." (Exodus 15:16).

But we Your people, who You purchased with your pure Blood, may we be the subject of the psalm, "Remember Your congregation, which You have purchased of old, the tribe of Your inheritance, which You have redeemed—This Mount Zion where You have dwelt. (Psalm 74:2)

"And He brought them to His holy border, this mountain which His right hand had acquired." (Psalm 78:54)

In our saying, "we know none other but You", our consciences must be rebuked for we actually know other foreign gods such as money, people, status and power. When we say "we know non other but you, we must reflect on our actions, for our entire reliance must be on our God, according to the Holy Bible:

"I have hated those who regard useless idols; but I trust in the Lord" (Psalm 31:6).

"Many sorrows shall be to the wicked; but he who trusts in the Lord, mercy shall surround him" (Psalm 32:10).

"Oh, taste and see that the Lord is good; blessed is the man who trusts in Him!" (Psalm 34:8).

"Trust in the Lord with all your heart, and lean not on your own understanding" (Proverbs 3:5).

"Your holy name we utter"… that is, we know no other name but Your Holy name, which is called upon us as Christians. "Nor is there salvation in any other, for there is no other name under heaven given among men by which we must be saved" (Acts 4:12).

"May our souls live by Your holy Spirit"… because your Holy Spirit is the source of the true life, and whoever does not live by the Holy Spirit is dead even if he has the appearance of one who lives. "I know your works, that you have a name that you are alive, but you are dead" (Revelations 3:1)

"and let not the death of sins have dominion over us, we Your servants, nor over all Your people". Rather let us have strength in You to defeat all the power of the enemy, the dominion of sin and death

Secondly, Litany of Fathers

We pray in the Litany of Fathers for His Holiness the pope, for the metropolitans, bishops and for all the clergy. This indicates that the faction that needs the most prayers in the Church are the clergy. This is because the church recognises the position and the responsibilities of the fathers, and knows the extent of the spiritual warfare cast by the devil who follows the principle of, "I strike the Shepherd and the sheep of the flock will be scattered" (Matthew 26:31)

This is why we pray for the Pope, the bishop, the priests and all the servants. This is what our teacher St Paul the Apostle has asked of us:

"you also helping together in prayer for us, that thanks may be given by many persons on [a]our behalf for the gift granted to us through many" (2 Corinthians 1:11).

"Brethren, pray for us" (1 Thessalonians 5:25).

"Finally, brethren, pray for us, that the word of the Lord may run swiftly and be glorified, just as it is with you" (2 Thessalonians 3:1)

"Pray for us; for we are confident that we have a good conscience, in all things desiring to live honorably" (Hebrews 13:18).

All of this is in accordance with the Biblical principle:

"and pray for one another…The effective, fervent prayer of a righteous man avails much" (James 5:16).

"praying always with all prayer and supplication in the Spirit, being watchful to this end with all perseverance and supplication for all the saints" (Ephesians 6:18)

"meanwhile praying also for us, that God would open to us a door for the word, to speak the mystery of Christ, for which I am also in chains" (Colossians 4:3)

The naming of the Pope and the bishop during the liturgy is the attestation of the Orthodoxy of the church and her belonging. Similarly, it corroborates the Orthodoxy of the priest who is praying, that he is not separated from the universal church which is represented by the Pope and the bishop. Naming the pope and the bishop also shows that the parish priest does not conduct a liturgical service independent of his bishop, with further attests to the unity of the church. We also mention the names of the patriarchs of our sister churches like the Syriac, Eritrean and Ethiopian, to demonstrate the universality of the church and its unity in the faith.

The priest prays for the Pope, saying, "rightly handling the word of truth, shepherding Your people in purity and righteousness, and all the orthodox bishops, hegumens, priests, and deacons, and all the fullness of Your one, only, holy, catholic and apostolic Church". Here, the prayer emphasizes that the Pope and the bishops of the holy Church should follow correct interpretation and practice upright shepherding.

When we mention all the Orthodox bishops, we mean those who are not heretics, that is, those who preserve the faith and have not deviated. The word "Orthodox" does not mean bias towards the Orthodox Church only but signifies adherence to the quality of faith. The term (Orthodoxy) carries two meanings: the Church's title and a description of the faith. The word originally described the faith, then over time, it became a title and a name for the Church that adheres to the orthodoxy of faith. It is not zealotry but adherence to the straight faith.

There is a semantic association between the words "Orthodox" and "Bishops". This is because the bishop leads the Church and is responsible for the sound teaching in it. "Take heed to yourself and to the doctrine. Continue in them, for in doing this you will save both yourself and those who hear you" (1 Timothy 4:16). If the bishop is Orthodox, then the priest, deacons, and subdeacons are also Orthodox. He is the head of teaching in the Church. "As I urged you when I went into Macedonia—remain in Ephesus that you may charge some that they teach no other doctrine" (1 Timothy 1:3).

Then the priest continues, saying, "Grant them and us peace and safety in every place. Their prayers which they offer on our behalf (and on behalf of Your people) as well as ours on their behalf". Here, the priest holds the incense box and points with it towards the congregation because the incense represents prayers and is an expression of fellowship. It's as if the priest is involving the people in prayers, with him, for him and for the bishop and pope. Then he places a spoonful of incense after this in the censer while saying, "receive them upon Your holy, rational altar in heaven, as a sweet savor of incense".

Just as the incense fills the church with a pleasant fragrance, so do the prayers of the people for the fathers fill the church with a fragrant aroma. We pray and say in one of the prayers, "give splendour to the clergy," so that the fragrance of the church is a pleasing and beautiful aroma. For when we pray for them, our prayers become an aroma of incense on the rational, heavenly altar. Thus the church becomes filled with truth, faith and purity.

Then the priest continues, saying, "All their enemies, visible and invisible, trample and humiliate under their feet speedily". This has been mentioned in the Book of Revelation: "Indeed I will make those of the synagogue of Satan, who say they are Jews and are not, but lie—indeed I will make them come and worship before your feet, and to know that I have loved you" (Revelation 3:9). Therefore, this is a promise from God that the enemies of the Church will be subdued under the feet of the fathers.

The priest then says, "As for them, keep them in peace righteousness in Your holy Church." We truly need God to preserve the leaders of the Church in peace and righteousness; peace among themselves, peace with the people, and peace with those outside. Their leadership in the church should be characterized by truth, justice, and fairness, because the priest, and more so the bishop, is a judge and a father at the same time. Everyone turns to him for advice and the resolution of problems and disputes. Therefore, he must be wise, patient, and just so that no one is weary of him.

We pray for them to receive these gifts:

The Patriarch or the bishop prays these prayers if present, saying, "Remember, O Lord, our assemblies. bless them, grant that they may be to us without obstacle or hindrance, that we may hold them according to Your holy and blessed will houses of prayer, houses of purity, houses of blessing. Grant them to us, O Lord, and to Your servants who will come after us, forever".

The assemblies we pray for are:

1. Liturgical assemblies: Public prayers like the Divine Liturgy.

2. Educational assemblies: Church education and youth meetings.

3. Administrative assemblies

4. Family assemblies: pastoral visitations

5. Personal assemblies: In confession sessions or individual work.

We seek blessings for all these assemblies so that we may achieve God's purpose through them and that they bring forth the desired fruits. The blessing we seek for the meetings is the blessing of the number of attendees, with no one absent, as the Scripture says: "Not forsaking the assembling of ourselves together, as is the manner of some, but exhorting one another, and so much the more as you see the Day approaching" (Hebrews 10:25). Also, the blessing of the success of the service offered in the assemblies because we are not merely concerned with the number of attendees but, more importantly, their spiritual benefit.

Without objection or hindrance:

The worst thing that could face the Church is to be prevented from holding its assemblies, especially the liturgical ones. In the past, the Church used to celebrate masses in caves, catacombs, tombs, and deserts during times of persecution when meetings were restricted. Therefore, we pray that our good God does not allow times when church meetings are prohibited. May we not be deprived of liturgical prayers, hearing the word of God in preaching, and ecclesiastical teaching.

This prayer reminds us that we should not neglect our assemblies as long as there is an opportunity to attend. Our forefathers endured difficult times, and they longed for the chance to participate in communal prayers but it was not available to them.

In the early days, the apostles gathered in houses before churches were built.

- "So continuing daily with one accord in the temple, and breaking bread from house to house, they ate their food with gladness and simplicity of heart" (Acts 2:46).

"And daily in the temple, and in every house, they did not cease teaching and preaching Jesus as the Christ" (Acts 5:42).

Beloved Lord Jesus, grant, O Lord, that there be no obstacle or hindrance that prevents me from enjoying the fellowship of the Church in prayers and liturgies… neither external or internal obstacle, nor sickness, preoccupation, laziness or because of sin that veils Your face from me, making me ashamed to face You in prayer. Nor hindrance arising from disturbances in the country's security and peace, nor due to wars, famines, or natural disasters. Wherever I am allowed to travel for any reason, I hope there is a church where I can take refuge. May I not be deprived of the companionship of prayer and partaking in Your divine mysteries.

The holy and blessed will of God

We pray that we "may hold them according to Your holy and blessed will", as we ought to hold our assemblies. Some resort to strange methods of attracting congregants such as financial incentives, gifts, and wow-factors. These methods indicate the absence of God's Spirit in the service, and the success of these meetings relies on human methods. This is contrary to what our teacher St Paul the Apostle said, "But we have this treasure in earthen vessels, that the excellence of the power may be of God and not of us" (2 Corinthians 4:7). We must say to God, "You, O Lord, are the one who makes the meeting strong and according to your will."

Turning to temptations and incentives to make our meetings successful is a declaration of spiritual bankruptcy. True success is always built on God's work in His church.

- "For we are God's fellow workers; you are God's field, you are God's building" (1 Corinthians 3:9).

- "For it is God who works in you both to will and to do for His good pleasure" (Philippians 2:13).

- "I planted, Apollos watered, but God gave the increase" (1 Corinthians 3:6).

- "So then neither he who plants is anything, nor he who waters, but God who gives the increase" (1 Corinthians 3:5).

Our teacher Paul the Apostle preached the Christ crucified against the current and succeeded in his service because it was carried out by the Spirit of God.

- "For Jews request a sign, and Greeks seek after wisdom; but we preach Christ crucified, to the Jews a stumbling block and to the Greeks foolishness!" (1 Corinthians 1:22-23).

"not with wisdom of words, lest the cross of Christ should be made of no effect." (1 Corinthians 1:17)

- "And I, brethren, when I came to you, did not come with excellence of speech or of wisdom declaring to you the testimony of God. For

I determined not to know anything among you except Jesus Christ and Him crucified. I was with you in weakness, in fear, and in much trembling. And my speech and my preaching were not with persuasive words of human wisdom, but in demonstration of the Spirit and of power, that your faith should not be in the wisdom of men but in the power of God." (1 Corinthians 2:1-5).

The Secret of Success in Meetings:

I truly believe that the secret of the success of our meetings in the Coptic Church is not in eloquence, preparations, attendance, visitations, gifts, or any means of incentivisation or attraction. The secret of its success is in these litanies that we pray, saying, "Grant that they may be to us without obstacle or hindrance, that we may hold them according to Your holy and blessed will". The Holy Spirit works through the most meagre resources when we pray and brings forth the greatest fruits through His works.

Christian meetings were officially prohibited by governments in many eras, and people were forced to gather in underground places, in tombs or in cemeteries to pray in very difficult conditions. These meetings, completely devoid of any incentives or factors of fascination, were very successful, producing saints, martyrs, and true theologians. The Church truly lived through the power of the prayer of this beautiful litany, and its assemblies were truly according to God's holy and blessed will. May we also follow in this way by His grace.

Purity of Teaching:

"According to the will of God" also means: the integrity of the ideas presented in these assemblies. Because God's will is for us to know His mind, in truth, not according to what appeases the people. Therefore, our teacher Paul the Apostle alerts everyone entrusted with teaching in the Holy Church to uphold integrity, "in doctrine showing integrity, reverence, incorruptibility" (Titus 2:7). Teaching in the Church is the delivery of the correct, true, and orthodox faith, "the faith which was once for all delivered to the saints" (Jude 1: 3). The Church is keen on protecting this teaching from distortion and change.

- "Yet you obeyed from the heart that form of doctrine to which you were delivered" (Romans 6:17).

- "Stay away from all believers who live idle lives and don't follow the tradition they received from us" (2 Thessalonians 3:6).

"If you instruct the brethren in these things, you will be a good minister of Jesus Christ, nourished in the words of faith and of the good doctrine which you have carefully followed" (1 Timothy 4:6).

- "If anyone teaches otherwise and does not consent to wholesome words, even the words of our Lord Jesus Christ, and to the doctrine which accords with godliness, he is proud, knowing nothing, but is obsessed with disputes and arguments over words, from which come envy, strife, reviling, evil suspicions, useless wranglings of men of corrupt minds and destitute of the truth, who suppose that godliness is a means of gain. From such withdraw yourself. Now godliness with contentment is great gain" (1 Timothy 6:3-5).

- "For the time will come when they will not endure sound doctrine, but according to their own desires, because they have itching ears, they will heap up for themselves teachers" (2 Timothy 4:3).

Therefore, it is written regarding the qualifications of the chosen bishop for this noble rank:

- "Holding fast the faithful word as he has been taught, that he may be able, by sound doctrine, both to exhort and convict those who contradict" (Titus 1:9).

- "But as for you, teach what accords with sound doctrine" (Titus 2:1).

- "If anyone comes to you and does not bring this teaching, do not receive him into your house or give him any greeting" (2 John 1:10).

Houses of Prayer:

The liturgical prayers are not limited to the assemblies in the church, but we also pray for our Christian homes saying, "houses of prayer, houses of purity, houses of blessing". This is a beautiful ladder established by the Church. When we begin with prayer, we attain purity, and consequently, our lives are filled with blessings.

The word "houses" here refers to both churches and the homes of believers. Whoever wants his house to be blessed must gather his children and wife, pray together even just once a day in the evening, and read a chapter from the Holy Bible. This sacred family meeting will fill the house with peace, harmony, love, and the purity of life. Consequently, the blessings of heaven will descend, and the house will be a true church, as the Scriptures say, "the church in your house" (Philemon 1:2).

During the recitation of this phrase in the liturgy, the priest censes with the censer above the chalice the sign of the cross, as if drawing strength from the precious blood to fill our homes with prayer, purity, and blessing.

Continuity of Generations:

"Grant them to us, O Lord, and to Your servants who will come after us, forever". This is a beautiful way to preserve continuity of the Church across all generations. Today, we pray for future generations, while the prayers of previous generations continue to resonate in the ears of heaven, supporting and strengthening us.

Idol Worship:

Then the priest prays: "The worship of idols, utterly uproot from the world. Satan and all his powers trample and humiliate them under our feet speedily. The offences and their instigators, abolish. Let the dissensions of corrupt heresies cease. The enemies of Your holy Church, O Lord, as at all times, now also humiliate".

Some may think that idol worship has ended in the world, or at least in Egypt. But we must know that it still exists in new forms. Money is a new idol worshipped by people, and they seek its validation. They can even take sinful paths to obtain it, disregarding the divine commandments. Truly, Jesus said: "No one can serve two masters, for either he will hate the one and love the other, or he will be devoted to the one and despise the other. You cannot serve God and money" (Matthew 6:24).

It's not just money; desires, bad friends, and all kinds of sins can be idols. We pray that God eradicates all remnants of idol worship from the world, crushes Satan under the feet of believers, and protects them from the dominion of sin, evil, and temptation. May the believers always be victorious and triumphant by His grace.

- "Resist the devil, and he will flee from you" (James 4:7).

- "Be sober-minded; be watchful. Your adversary the devil prowls around like a roaring lion, seeking someone to devour" (1 Peter 5:8).

- "And I saw something like a sea of glass mingled with fire, and those who have the victory over the beast, over his image and over his mark and over the number of his name, standing on the sea of glass, having harps of God" (Revelation 15:2).

Under the category of idol worship are practices based on deviant beliefs, such as worship of Satan, magic, witchcraft, resorting to fortune-tellers, and demonic activities, and other similar practices that people fall into either out of ignorance or with pre-meditated will.

The offences and their instigators

The heretics are the instigators of offences. Many times, people live in the simplicity of faith and spiritual practice until a heretic comes and corrupts the simplicity of their minds. He introduces doubts and philosophies that rob faith of its purity and simplicity. The Church is then forced into a spiritual intellectual struggle against these imposters and doubters to explain and establish pure faith in the hearts of believers.

"I fear, lest somehow, as the serpent deceived Eve by his craftiness, so your minds may be corrupted from the simplicity that is in Christ" (2 Corinthians 11:3).

The first enemies of the Church are the heretics. They are more dangerous to the Church than rulers who exert all their efforts to fight against faith. Rulers may come and go, but the Church remains. History does not tell us of a ruler who stood against the Church and died a normal death. Therefore, the Church does not fear rulers as enemies of faith, but heretics are the true enemies of the Church. Heresies are also the work of Satan. Hence, we pray: "the offences and their instigators, abolish. Let the dissensions of their heresies cease". This refers to ending the divisions caused by corrupt heresies.

Heresies are a form of idol worship because they rebel against faith and resist God and the Church.

"For rebellion is as the sin of witchcraft, and stubbornness is as iniquity and idolatry" (1 Samuel 15:23). They are the tares sown by the enemy among the wheat to spoil the sacred harvest. Therefore, we pray, "the enemies of Your holy Church, O Lord, as at all times, now also humiliate".

There is not a heretic who stood against the Church, since the times of our fathers the apostles till now, that has remained. For whoever wishes to preserve his peace and safety ought to preserve his faith.

The enemies of faith are not only heretics but also anyone who fights against Christian faith and opposes apostolic submission. This includes those who try to tarnish the purity of church life from within or outside the church.

"Strip their vanity", for the core of heresy is vanity. The humble person listens to the teaching and corrects his thoughts, however the proud person believes that they are correct and do not accept any revisions or corrections from others. Therefore, whoever opposes the church, thinks they are more powerful than God, who is her protector, keeper and groom.

"Show them their weakness speedily". The enemies of the church always feel like they are more powerful than God Himself, and that the divine hand of justice cannot touch them. Thus, they commit savagery, injustice and murder with no accountability. However, the powerful hand of God appears quickly, and avenges his beloved children who have tasted bitterness for the love of His holy name… "since it is a righteous thing with God to repay with tribulation those who trouble you" (2 Thessalonians 1:6).

"Bring to naught their envies, their intrigues, their madness, and their wickedness, and their slanders, which they commit against us". For these are the vile methods utilised by the heretics, which befit them. These are the devices that they used with St Stephen when they talked with him and could not rebut his convincing answers, "Then they secretly induced men to say, "We have heard him speak blasphemous words against Moses and God" (Acts 6:11). This is because "they were not able to resist the wisdom and the Spirit by which he spoke" (Acts 6:10).

The weakness of the enemies of the church and their lack of logic makes them resort to these cheap tactics and lies. Thus, the Lord Christ said about them, "You are of your father the devil, and the desires of your father you want to do. He was a murderer from the beginning, and does not stand in the truth, because there is no truth in him. When he speaks a lie, he speaks from his own resources, for he is a liar and the father of it".

The church prays for those saying, "show them their weakness speedily", for the Church does not lose hope in their return, praying for them to realise their weakness, for if they knew their weakness they would return.

"Bring them all to no avail. Disperse their counsel, O God, who dispersed the counsel of Ahithophel". Make these enemies as if they do not exist, so that the Church is not hindered. Turn their evils into good because you are the one who creates goodness and does not accept evil. Just as you did with Joseph so he said to his brothers: "you meant evil against me; but God meant it for good, in order to bring it about as it is this day, to save many people alive" (Genesis 50:20). Let every counsel they plot against the Church rebound on them, as it happened with Ahithophel's counsel against David.

"Arise, O Lord God, let all Your enemies be scatter, and let all who hate Your holy name flee before Your face". The first person who said this petition was Moses the prophet, ""So it was, whenever the ark set out, that Moses said: "Rise up, O LORD! Let Your enemies be scattered, And let those who hate You flee before You" (Numbers 10:35).

This prayer was also made by Solomon the wise on the day of the consecration of the temple, "Arise, O LORD God, to Your resting place, You and the ark of Your strength. Let Your priests, O LORD God, be clothed with salvation, And let Your saints rejoice in goodness" (2 Chronicles 6:41).

"Arise, O Lord! Save me, O my God! For you have struck all my enemies on the cheekbone; you have broken the teeth of the ungodly" (Psalm 3:7).

"Arise, O Lord, in Your anger; Lift Yourself up because of the rage of my enemies; Rise up for me to the judgment You have commanded!" (Psalm 7:6).

"Arise, O LORD, Do not let man prevail; Let the nations be judged in Your sight" (Psalm 9:19).

"Arise, O LORD! O God, lift up Your hand! Do not forget the humble" (Psalm 10:12).

"Arise, O LORD, Confront him, cast him down; Deliver my life from the wicked with Your sword" (Psalm 17:13).

Arise, O Lord, why do you sleep? Arise and scatter all the evildoers. Let all who gather against you be dispersed. Show your strength with your arm, "in order that the living may know that the Most High rules in the kingdom of men, gives it to whomever He will, and sets over it the lowest of men" (Daniel 4:17), "for they shall soon be cut down like the grass, and wither as the green herb" (Psalm 37:2).

And the priest continues, "But let Your people be in blessing, thousands of thousands and ten thousand times ten thousand, doing Your will". The priest says this phrase while censing with the censer towards the people when he says, "thousands and thousands, ten thousand times ten thousand," not only for their multitude but that they may do the will of God.

Prayers for the Place

In the Litany of the Place, we pray for the salvation of the world and every city we dwell in. By salvation we mean deliverance from tribulations, problems, plagues, famines and wars. This is why we say in the litany, "save us all from famine, plague, earthquake, drowning, fire, captivity by barbarians, the sword of the stranger, and the rising up of heretics."

The church prays for the city, even if it is a place of captivity or exile, following the words of the Scripture, "and seek the peace of the city where I have caused you to be carried away captive, and pray to the Lord for it; for in its peace you will have peace" (Jeremiah 29:7).

The church considers all places and cities as belonging to the Lord: "The earth is the LORD's, and all its fullness, The world and those who dwell therein" (Psalm 24:1).

Therefore, we say in the prayer, "Remember, O Lord, this Your holy place", for every place is for the Lord, and is thus a holy place which is sanctified by prayer; "for it is sanctified by the word of God and prayer" (1 Timothy 4:5).

Prayer protects the city from all evil, "In that day this song will be sung in the land of Judah: "We have a strong city; God will appoint salvation for walls and bulwarks" (Isaiah 26:1). This is because we believe that "Unless the Lord builds the house, They labor in vain who build it; Unless the Lord guards the city, The watchman stays awake in vain" (Psalm 127:1). We believe that the presence of faithful praying people protects the country from many disasters, "By the blessing of the upright the city is exalted, But it is overthrown by the mouth of the wicked. (Proverbs 11:11) "For I will defend this city, to save it for My own sake and for My servant David's sake" (Isaiah

37:35). "I will deliver you and this city from the hand of the king of Assyria, and I will defend this city" (Isaiah 38:6).

We pray not only for our city but for the whole world, praying for all places, cities, countries, villages and all their adornment (that is, the farms and fields surrounding the villages), and monasteries (the dwelling of our orthodox fathers).

The remarkable thing about these prayers is that they consider the rise of heretics as one of the causes of disturbance in the city. Heretics create disturbance and division, not less dangerous than the persecution of enemies of faith to the church, "looking carefully lest anyone fall short of the grace of God; lest any root of bitterness springing up cause trouble, and by this many become defiled" (Hebrews 12:15). "For rebellion is as the sin of witchcraft, and stubbornness is as iniquity and idolatry" (1 Samuel 15:23).

Therefore, it is also said, "If anyone comes to you and does not bring this doctrine, do not receive him into your house nor greet him" (2 John 1:10).

"But we command you, brethren, in the name of our Lord Jesus Christ, that you withdraw from every brother who walks disorderly and not according to the tradition which he received from us" (2 Thessalonians 3:6). Thus, the church prays for the destruction of the opposing, as their rise causes disturbance in the country.

Prayers for the King (Head of State)

The church also prays for the rulers, saying: "Remember O Lord the king (leader) of our land, Your servant … keep him in peace, righteousness, and strength. May all the barbarians, the nations that desire wars against all our prosperity be subdued unto him. Speak to his heart concerning the peace of Your one only holy catholic and apostolic Church. Grant him to think peaceably toward us and toward Your holy name that we too may lead a quiet and peaceful life, and may be found dwelling in all godliness and all dignity in You".

This prayer is an implementation of the scriptural command: "Therefore I exhort first of all that supplications, prayers, intercessions, and giving of thanks be made for all men, for kings and all who are in authority, that we may lead a quiet and peaceable life in all godliness and reverence" (1 Timothy 2:1-2),. For in the king's peace, there is peace for the kingdom and the church, "In the light of the king's face is life, And his favor is like a cloud of the latter rain" (Proverbs 16:15). The opposite is also true: "As messengers of death is the king's wrath, But a wise man will appease it" (Proverbs 16:14).

The Church teaches us obedience to rulers, not out of submission and weakness, but out of respect and support. "Let every soul be subject to the governing authorities. For there is no authority except from God, and the authorities that exist are appointed by God. Therefore whoever resists the authority resists the ordinance of God, and those who resist will bring judgment on themselves. For rulers are not a terror to good works, but to evil. Do you want to be unafraid of the authority? Do what is good, and you will have praise from the same. For he is God's minister to you for good. But if you do evil, be afraid; for he does not bear the sword in vain; for he is God's minister, an avenger to execute wrath on him who practices evil. Therefore you must be subject, not only because of wrath but also for conscience' sake. For because of this you also pay taxes, for they are God's ministers attending continually to this very thing. Render therefore to all their due: taxes to whom taxes are due, customs to whom customs, fear to whom fear, honor to whom honor" (Romans 13:1-7).

Our teacher Paul the apostle, further reiterates this Christian virtue in his letter to his disciple Titus, "Remind them to be subject to rulers and authorities, to obey, to be ready for every good work" (Titus 3:1).

Likewise, our teacher Peter emphasises he same guidance: "Therefore, submit yourselves to every ordinance of man for the Lord's sake, whether to the king as supreme, or to governors, as to those who are sent by him for the punishment of evildoers and for the praise of those who do good" (1 Peter 2:13-14).

This reflects a general direction in Christian thought to submit to authorities with awareness, humility, love, sincerity, and a heartfelt desire for the peace of the country we live in, understanding that authority is given by God to rulers, presidents, and governors. "You could have no power at all against Me unless it had been given you from above" (John 19:11). "The king's heart is in the hand of the Lord, like the rivers of water; He turns it wherever He wishes" (Proverbs 21:1).

The Church doesn't only pray for rulers and presidents but also for all those working in the state: "Remember, o lord, our brethren, the orthodox believers who are in the palace (government) and all who are in the military".

In the deacon's litany, it is said: "Pray that Christ our God may grant us mercy and compassion before the ruling authorities, and soften their heart toward us for that which is good at all times, and forgive us our sins". These prayers express the true Christian spirit which wishes goodness on every one, including the rulers, even if they are persecuting the Church and the believers.

Litany of the Air of Heaven, the Fruits and the Waters

TThe Holy Church does not forget to pray for the material needs of people. It prays for water, air, fruits, and crops, asking Christ our God to bless them so that people may be satisfied, and there may be no famines threatening their lives and peace.

The Church connects these natural needs with the spiritual concerns of people. Poverty, hunger, and natural disasters distract people from holy spiritual works. Therefore, we pray, "that we too having sufficiency in everything always, may abound in every good deed." This prayer reminds us of what is stated in the Book of Proverbs: "Give me neither poverty nor riches—feed me with the food allotted to me; lest I be full and deny You, and say, 'Who is the Lord?' Or lest I be poor and steal, and profane the name of my God" (Proverbs 30:8-9).

The Church prays for water during the Nile flood, saying: "Remember, O Lord, the waters of the rivers in this year, bless them, raise them to their measure according to Your grace". The rising of water to its measure gives an opportunity for crops to grow appropriately. If the water is less than the measure, it leads to famine, and if it exceeds the measure, it causes disasters such as floods.

The Church prays not only for Egypt but for all rivers in the world because the Church is a mother to the whole world, responsible for the salvation of all. The Church prays for crops during the sowing season and for fruits during the harvest season. As for our churches in the diaspora, they pray for the three types of litanies throughout the year due to the diversity and multiplicity of seasons in each country according to its climatic conditions.

The Church considers the rise of water to its measure a cause of joy for the face of the earth, as stated in the prophecy of the Prophet Isaiah, "The wilderness and the wasteland shall be glad for them, and the desert shall rejoice and blossom as the rose. It shall blossom abundantly and rejoice, even with joy and singing" (Isaiah 35:1-2).

We can consider the earth as our hearts, which need the water of the Holy Spirit to be satisfied, to flourish, and to bear fruit for the glory of God. "For the fruit of the Spirit is in all goodness, righteousness, and truth" (Ephesians 5:9). "May its furrows be abundantly watered and its fruits be plentiful". We care primarily about the fruits of the Spirit, and our eternal life. Still, this doesn't prevent us from asking God for our temporal needs, especially as there are promises from God of special blessings for His people if they walk in His commandments and judgments:

"So you shall serve the Lord your God, and He will bless your bread and your water. And I will take sickness away from the midst of you" (Exodus 23:25).

"And He will love you and bless you and multiply you; He will also bless the fruit of your womb and the fruit of your land, your grain and your new wine and your oil, the increase of your cattle and the offspring of your flock, in the land of which He swore to your fathers to give you" (Deuteronomy 7:13).

"Because the Lord your God will bless you in all your produce and in all the work of your hands, so that you surely rejoice" (Deuteronomy 16:15).

Thus, temporal blessings are also an indication of the Lord's blessing for our lives and His satisfaction with His people. Therefore, we pray fervently for these blessings.

"Bless the crown of the year with Your goodness". Here, perhaps, we echo the psalm: "You visit the earth and water it, You greatly enrich it; the river of God is full of water; You provide their grain, For so You have prepared it. You water its ridges abundantly, You settle its furrows; You make it soft with showers, You bless its growth. You crown the year with Your goodness, and Your paths drip with abundance. They drop on the pastures of the wilderness, and the little hills rejoice on every side. The pastures are clothed with flocks; the valleys also are covered with grain; they shout for joy, they also sing" (Psalm 65:9-13).

The Church implores the face of God for the sake of the poor, widows, orphans, traveller and stranger because "He administers justice for the fatherless and the widow, and loves the stranger, giving him food and clothing." (Deuteronomy 10:18). He has instructed us to serve these vulnerable groups, "When you reap your harvest in your field, and forget a sheaf in the field, you shall not go back to get it; it shall be for the stranger, the fatherless, and the widow, that the Lord your God may bless you in all the work of your hands. When you beat your olive trees, you shall not go over the boughs again; it shall be for the stranger, the fatherless, and the widow. When you gather the grapes of your vineyard, you shall not glean it afterward; it shall be for the stranger, the fatherless, and the widow." (Deuteronomy 24:19-21).

Moreover, He set a severe punishment for those who oppress widows, orphans, and strangers:

"Cursed is the one who perverts the justice due the stranger, the fatherless, and widow" (Deuteronomy 27:19). As for guests, God has commanded us to serve them with joy:

"distributing to the needs of the saints, given to hospitality" (Romans 12:13).

"Do not forget to entertain strangers, for by so doing some have unwittingly entertained angels" (Hebrews 13:2).

"As each one has received a gift, minister it to one another, as good stewards of the manifold grace of God" (1 Peter 4:10).

Consequently, it is not fitting for us to implore the heart of God for the poor, widows, orphans, travellers, and strangers, and then neglect their service after obtaining blessings from God through them.

The litany continues, saying, "and for the sake of all of us who entreat You and seek Your holy name". Not only the poor need God, but we all do because we cannot live without His assistance, as He said: "For without Me, you can do nothing" (John 15:5). Truly, O Lord Jesus, we seek You and implore Your divine gifts at all times.

"Lord, to whom shall we go?" (John 6:68).

"For the eyes of everyone wait upon You, for You give them their food in due season":

"For the eyes of all look to You, and You give them their food at the proper time. "The eyes of all look expectantly to You, and You give them their food in due season. You open Your hand and satisfy the desire of every living thing" (Psalm 145:15-16).

Indeed, blessed are the people who have such a God! "Happy are the people whose God is the Lord!" (Psalm 144:15).

"Deal with us according to Your goodness, O Giver of food to all flesh. "Who gives food to all flesh,

For His mercy endures forever" (Psalm 136:25).

"Fill our hearts with joy and gladness":

"Nevertheless He did not leave Himself without witness, in that He did good, gave us rain from heaven and fruitful seasons, filling our hearts with food and gladness" (Acts 14:17).

"So that we, also, having all sufficiency in everything, may abound in every good work. "And God is able to make all grace abound toward you, that you, always having all sufficiency in all things, may have an abundance for every good work" (2 Corinthians 9:8).

The Church teaches us to seek contentment: "Give us this day our daily bread" (Matthew 6:11). We learn this from our teacher, the Apostle Paul, who said "Not that I speak in regard to need, for I have learned in whatever state I am, to be content: I know how to be abased, and I know how to abound. Everywhere and in all things I have learned both to be full and to be hungry, both to abound and to suffer need." (Philippians 4:12).

This spiritual principle makes us untroubled in anything: "Be anxious for nothing, but in everything by prayer and supplication, with thanksgiving, let your requests be made known to God" (Philippians 4:6).

The merciful God fulfills all our needs abundantly, "And my God shall supply all your need according to His riches in glory by Christ Jesus." (Philippians 4:19).

Litany of the servants of the church

The servants of the Church need the prayers of all believers for them to be supported by our God in their service, that they may complete their struggle in the Church without reproach, as our teacher Paul the Apostle says, "We give no offense in anything, that our ministry may not be blamed" (2 Corinthians 6:3).

Therefore, the Church prays continuously, saying: "Give splendour to the clergy" (servants who are consecrated to serve the Church in the orders of the diaconate, priesthood, and episcopacy).

Our teacher Paul asked for these prayers for himself:

"finally, brethren, pray for us, that the word of the Lord may run swiftly and be glorified, just as it is with you" (2 Thessalonians 3:1).

"You also helping together in prayer for us, that thanks may be given by many persons on our behalf for the gift granted to us through many" (2 Corinthians 1:11).

After praying for the Pope and bishops, the Church raises prayers for the rest of the ecclesiastical ranks, saying, "and those who rightly handle the word of truth with him (the pope), grant them unto Your holy Church to shepherd Your flock in peace".

We must contemplate on this characteristic that distinguishes the servants of the Church, that is "rightly handling the word of truth": "Do your best to present yourself to God as one approved, a worker who does not need to be ashamed and who correctly handles the word of truth." (2 Timothy 2:15).

"Handles" here means "interpreter, guider, and teacher". Therefore, teaching in the Church should be straightforward without deviations, according to the specifications explained by our teacher, the Apostle Paul, when he said, "For the appeal we make does not spring from error or impure motives, nor are we trying to trick you. On the contrary, we speak as those approved by God to be entrusted with the gospel" (1 Thessalonians 2:3-4). Our teacher Paul the Apostle also advised his disciple Titus with the same guidance, saying, "In doctrine showing integrity, reverence, incorruptibility" (Titus 2:7). Additionally, he also said, "Take heed to yourself and to the doctrine. Continue in them, for in doing this you will save both yourself and those who hear you" (1 Timothy 4:16).

One of the most important features of sound teaching is honesty with oneself, avoiding hypocrisy, and speaking beliefs clearly. This is what our teacher, the Apostle Paul, means by the word "impure motives". Therefore, he described his disciples as being straightforward in faith: "to Timothy, my true son in the faith" (1 Timothy 1:2) and "to Titus, my true son in our common faith" (Titus 1:4).

The Church cries out in every liturgy for God to send laborers to His harvest and prays that they may be competent and faithful to the faith, "You therefore, my son, be strong in the grace that is in Christ Jesus. And the things that you have heard from me among many witnesses, commit these to faithful men who will be able to teach others also" (2 Timothy 2:2).

Indeed, O my good God, bless Your holy Church with such people in every country, village, valley, and street, and grant faithful individuals who are capable of teaching Your people with Your pure teaching without deviation in every church and on every pulpit for the sake of the integrity of the faith— that was "once for all entrusted to God's holy people" (Jude 1:3).

When the faith and the teaching are upright and true, the congregation are shepherded in peace. However, the people are derailed when the current of heresies and western ideologies enters the church.

It is noticeable when a local church has priests who have the spirit of discernment and distinction, genuine fatherhood, a sound Orthodox sense. For you will find this church thriving in peace and producing a multitude of saints.

Unfortunately, if the local church lacks this enlightened fatherhood, then strangers might creep in under the false pretext of reviving the church with unusual methods and teachings. This causes the Church to lose its identity. It becomes without defined characteristics, no longer Orthodox, nor non-Orthodox! It has lost its flavor and distinctiveness, becoming unclear in vision, and its service collapses, leading to divisions, disturbances, and lack of spiritual productivity.

This type of servant or priest influenced by these unusual methods may imagine that he has brought about a spiritual revival in the Church and caused an increase in the number of people!! However, the proof is always in the final result and the outcome of the service.

The local church that does not adhere to the spirit of the fathers in prayer, worship, liturgy, teaching, and service in general, cannot produce saints and nor present souls ready to bear witness and die for the name of Christ.

This is why the Holy Bible warned us saying, "looking carefully lest anyone fall short of the grace of God; lest any root of bitterness springing up cause trouble, and by this many become defiled" (Hebrews 12:15).

Therefore, the leader- the priest, and the service coordinator, and anyone who is responsible- must stand guard for upright teaching, always remembering the words of the Scripture:

"Guard what was committed to your trust, avoiding the profane and idle babblings and contradictions of what is falsely called knowledge" (1 Timothy 6:20).

"That good thing which was committed to you, keep by the Holy Spirit who dwells in us" (2 Timothy 1:14).

While we emphasise teaching, we must also not neglect spiritual shepherding and seeking everyone's salvation, "shepherding Your flock in peace".

"Shepherd the flock of God which is among you, serving as overseers, not by compulsion but willingly, not for dishonest gain but eagerly; nor as being lords over those entrusted to you, but being examples to the flock. And when the Chief Shepherd appears, you will receive the crown of glory that does not fade away" (1 Peter 5:2-4).

"Take heed to yourselves and to all the flock, among which the Holy Spirit has made you overseers, to shepherd the church of God which He purchased with His own blood" (Acts 20:28).

True care must be holistic, "Him we preach, warning every man and teaching every man in all wisdom, that we may present every man perfect in Christ Jesus" (Colossians 1:28). Crying out with Moses the Prophet, "not a hoof shall be left behind" (Exodus 10:26), meaning that no one is lost, but presenting everyone saying, "here am I and the children whom the Lord has given me!" (Isaiah 8:18). With a heart ablaze with love for the holy flock, the priest and the servants cry out with the Apostle Paul, saying, "For I could wish that I myself were accursed from Christ for my brethren, my countrymen according to the flesh" (Romans 9:3), because "who is weak, and I am not weak? Who is made to stumble, and I do not burn with indignation?" (2 Corinthians 11:29).

The responsibility of pastoral care is very serious, for the Lord seeks the blood of people from the hand of the servant, "when I say to the wicked, 'You shall surely die,' and you give him no warning, nor speak to warn the wicked from his wicked way, to save his life, that same wicked man shall die in his iniquity; but his blood I will require at your hand" (Ezekiel 3:18). Let us cry out with the psalmist, "Deliver me from the guilt of bloodshed, O God, The God of my salvation" (Psalm 51:14).

The servant, at any rank, who understands the extent of the responsibility and serves souls with awareness, spirituality, and appreciation, is a pillar in the church, bringing forth new and ancient treasures from his treasure chest. The new treasures are the ways of service, and the ancient ones are the authenticity of teaching because he is a good servant, and his treasure is good. "A good man out of the good treasure of his heart brings forth good things" (Matthew 12:35).

The true servant always feels unworthy in himself, "but we have this treasure in earthen vessels, that the excellence of the power may be of God and not of us" (2 Corinthians 4:7). "For it is God who works in you both to will and to do for His good pleasure" (Philippians 2:13).

Lord Jesus, I truly need the church to lift up constant prayers for me, that I may faithfully dedicate my life to this serious responsibility. I thank you, O my good God, for placing in the heart of the church this sacred regard to pray, and encouraging the people to pray for the servants in all ecclesiastical ranks.

The litany of the Clergy:

"Remember, O Lord, the orthodox hegumens, priests and deacons and all the servants, and all who are in virginity. After the Church prays for the pope and the bishops, she prays for the hegumens, priests, deacons and all the clergy. In the Cyrillian liturgy, there is an even more detailed litany for the clergy and servants, "remember O Lord… the… Orthodox bishops in all places, and the priests, the deacons, the subdeacons, the readers, the chanters, the exorcists, the monks, the virgins, the widows, the orphans, the ascetics, and the laity; those who are joined in wedlock and those who rear children;

those who said to us "remember us," and those who did not say this; those whom we know and those whom we do not know; our enemies and our loved ones, O God, have mercy upon them".

The word "clergy" is derived from the Greek word "kleronomia," meaning inheritance. It implies that the servants of the church in all ranks are the Lord's inheritance on earth, or in other words, their share and inheritance in this life is the Lord Himself. As the Lord spoke to Aaron and his sons, the lineage of priesthood, saying, "The Lord said to Aaron: You shall have no inheritance in their land, nor shall you have any portion among them. I am your portion and your inheritance among the children of Israel" (Numbers 18:20). "Therefore Levi has no portion nor inheritance with his brethren; the Lord is his inheritance, just as the Lord your God promised him" (Deuteronomy 10:9).

We pray for the "readers", meaning those who read the Holy Scriptures in the church. For the "chanters", those who specialize in chanting the church hymns with spirituality and mastery. For the "exorcists", those who read the Psalms over the heads of those afflicted with evil spirits to expel them. As well as, the monks, the virgins, the widows, the orphans, the ascetics, and the laity (those without ecclesiastical ranks), "and all the fullness of Your holy Church".

In another instance, the church prays for "those who are standing in this place," meaning those present for prayer with us, and for the rest of the Orthodox in every place, and for the houses of the believers, "and all those in virginity, and all the people and the servants".

We also pray for the captives, whether in wars, prisons, or those captured by sin. We say, "Remember, O Lord, those who dwell in the mountains and the caves," meaning the expelled and fugitives, "and our brethren, who are in captivity. Grant them a peaceful return unto their own". We also pray for the distressed for God to relieve their distress. This includes all other categories that have not been mentioned if they exist.

Indeed, the church does not neglect to pray for anyone, even those who have no one to remember them. The Church is concerned for the salvation of all, thus she wishes that all have upright Orthodox faith and lifestyles, "and he purity of all Your faithful people", to fulfill this precious salvation.

Purity of all your faithfull people:

Spiritual life requires purity of heart, body, and senses, as the Scriptures say: "Therefore, having these promises, beloved, let us cleanse ourselves from all filthiness of the flesh and spirit, perfecting holiness in the fear of God" (2 Corinthians 7:1). "For God did not call us to uncleanness, but in holiness" (1 Thessalonians 4:7). Without a love for holiness, and a hatred for impurity, we cannot establish a spiritual life with our Holy God

- "Holiness, without which no one will see the Lord" (Hebrews 12:14).

- "Be holy, for I am holy" (1 Peter 1:16).

- "incorruptibility makes us near to God" (Wisdom 6:20).

- "Present your members as slaves of righteousness for holiness" (Romans 6:19).

Litany of Mercy:

"Remember, O Lord, to have mercy upon us all". And the people cry out saying in response, "have mercy upon us, O God, the Father, the Pantocrator". We do not hesitate during the duration of the liturgy to seek mercy from our good and merciful God. In every litany, the people respond, "Lord, have mercy - Kyrie Eleyson. When the priest declares that the Lord will come on the last day to judge everyone according to their deeds, we cry out, "according to Your mercy, O Lord, and not according to our sins," because we know that judgment will be according to the actions of the person, as mentioned repeatedly in the Holy Scriptures.

"God will reward or punish every person for what that person has done" (Romans 2:6).

"And all the churches shall know that I am He who searches the minds and hearts. And I will give to each one of you according to your works" (Revelation 2:23).

"And I saw the dead, small and great, standing before God, and books were opened. And another book was opened, which is the Book of Life. And the dead were judged according to their works, by the things which were written in the books. The sea gave up the dead who were in it, and Death and Hades delivered up the dead who were in them. And they were judged, each one according to his works" (Revelation 20:12-13).

However, we also know that "God puts no trust in His saints, and the heavens are not pure in His sight" (Job 15:15), and our sins are known to Him, "if you, Lord, should mark iniquities, O Lord, who could stand? But there is forgiveness with You" (Psalm 130:3-4). No matter what righteous deeds we do, we are in desperate need of the mercy of the Lord, "when you have done all those things which you are commanded, say, 'We are unprofitable servants. We have done what was our duty to do'" (Luke 17:10).

Our Lord is merciful and compassionate. "The Lord is merciful and gracious, slow to anger and abounding in mercy" (Psalm 103:8). We cannot be saved without His mercy, so we earnestly seek it from now and in every liturgy, so that we may enjoy it on the last day. It is not fitting to ask God for mercy while not showing it to one another, as "judgment is without mercy to the one who has shown no mercy. Mercy triumphs over judgment" (James 2:13).

We are required to perform righteous deeds, alongside faith of course, and then earnestly plead for God's mercy, and show mercy towards each other. Only then will we have favor with Him on the day of His appearance, "Therefore we make it our aim, whether present or absent, to be well pleasing to Him" (2 Corinthians 5:9).

So we may hear the blessed voice, "well done, good and faithful servant! You have been faithful over a few things; I will make you ruler over many things. Enter into the joy of your Lord" (Matthew 25:21). "For I was hungry and you gave Me food; I was thirsty and you gave Me drink; I was a stranger and you took Me in; I was naked and you clothed Me; I was sick and you visited Me; I was in prison and you came to Me" (Matthew 25:35-36). "Amen. Even so, come, Lord Jesus" (Revelation 22:20).

Litany for the Catechumens

The Church prays a litany for the catechumens. In it the priest says, "Remember, O Lord, the catechumens of Your people; have mercy on them, confirm them in the faith in You. All traces of idolatry cast out of their heart. Your law, Your fear, Your commandments, Your truths, and Your holy ordinances, establish in their heart. Grant them that they may know the certainty of the words with which they have been instructed. At the appointed time, may they be worthy of the washing of the new birth, unto the forgiveness of their sins, preparing them to be a temple of Your Holy Spirit".

We pray this litany in the liturgical rite of baptism, as well as in the unction of the sick, the liturgy of the waters, the prostration, the feast of Pentecost and daily in the inaudible prayer of the Gospel in the divine liturgy.

The priest says, "Remember, O Lord, the catechumens of Your people; have mercy on them." They have not yet become part of the people of Christ or of His holy flock; this precious membership is obtained through baptism. "For by one Spirit we were all baptized into one body" (1 Corinthians 12:13). Yet the Church calls them "the catechumens of Your people." They have begun to be His people because they believed in His divinity. The deacon responds, saying, "Pray for the catechumens of our people, that the Lord may bless them and confirm them in the Orthodox Faith, to the last breath, and forgive us our sins."

They become "our people" through baptism, and we pray for them and on their behalf that the Lord may bless and establish them in what they have accepted, lest the devil deceive them and draw them to him again, losing their eternal salvation after putting their hands on the plow. "No one, having put his hand to the plow and looking back, is fit for the kingdom of God" (Luke 9:62).

The priest continues the litany, saying, "Establish them in the faith in You."

The Church is most concerned that these early sproutlings remain firm in faith and do not waver, stumble, or fall away, but continue to the end. "But he who endures to the end shall be saved" (Matthew 24:13). The crucial point is always at the end, not the beginning, as our teacher Paul rebuked the Galatians, saying, "Are you so foolish? Having begun in the Spirit, are you now being made perfect by the flesh?" (Galatians 3:3). Similarly, those of whom it was said, "for many walk, of whom I have told you often, and now tell you even weeping, that they are the enemies of the cross of Christ" (Philippians 3:18).

The priest concludes the litany, saying, "All traces of idolatry cast out of their hearts". Idol worship is not just bowing down to statues but includes all types of sin.

The Bible considers greed as a form of idol worship, "therefore put to death your members which are on the earth: fornication, uncleanness, passion, evil desire, and covetousness, which is idolatry" (Colossians 3:5), and as a model for sins that control a person, leading them into the domain of the devil and his debased worship, "God will reward or punish every person for what that person has done" (Romans 2:6).

The simplest sins, such as lying, are also a form of Satan worship, "You are of your father the devil, and the desires of your father you want to do. He was a murderer from the beginning, and does not stand in the truth, because there is no truth in him. When he speaks a lie, he speaks from his own resources, for he is a liar and the father of it" (John 8:44). "In this the children of God and the children of the devil are manifest: Whoever does not practice righteousness is not of God, nor is he who does not love his brother" (1 John 3:10).

After asking God to cast out all traces of idol worship from their hearts, we pray that Christ our God builds them in faith in a positive way, "Your law, Your fear, Your commandments, Your truths and Your holy ordinances, establish in their heart".

Faith is not complete without commitment to the commandments of Christ our God. He, in His glory, said, "Not everyone who says to Me, "Lord, Lord," shall enter the kingdom of heaven, but he who does the will of My Father in heaven" (Matthew 7:21). And the sign of love for Christ is to keep His commandments, "He who has My commandments and keeps them, it is he who loves Me" (John 14:21). "He who does not love Me does not keep My words" (John 14:24). It is not good for a person to come to baptism proclaiming love for Christ our God and then not adhere to His pure commandments.

Thus, how much more should we adhere to His pure commandments, having been born into the Christian faith, living in it thanks to the steadfastness of our faithful fathers and ancestors who did not succumb to any threat or temptation to leave the love of Christ and their faith in Him. We should follow in their footsteps, holding onto their faith and their sacred righteous behavior.

"Grant them that they may know the certainty of the words with which they have been instructed". 'certainty' in this quote means strength, validity, and surety, that it is a strong, unshaken, and confirmed faith.

"I make known to you, brethren, that the gospel which was preached by me is not according to man. For I neither received it from man, nor was I taught it, but it came through the revelation of Jesus Christ" (Galatians 1:11-12).

"And my speech and my preaching were not with persuasive words of human wisdom, but in demonstration of the Spirit and of power" (1 Corinthians 2:4).

"For our gospel did not come to you in word only, but also in power, and in the Holy Spirit, and in much assurance" (1 Thessalonians 1:5).

Our Christian faith is a sincere, sure, strong, and proven faith by the Holy Spirit and Its power.

"At the appointed time, may they be worthy of the washing of the new birth, unto forgiveness of their sins". The time in which they will receive the grace of baptism is determined by God, for 'To everything, there is a season, a time for every purpose under heaven' (Ecclesiastes 3:1).

The Church affirms here that the washing of the new birth is for the forgiveness of past sins through baptism, like the action of the flood that washed the earth from sin. As our teacher, the Apostle Peter, explained, "in which [the ark] a few, that is, eight souls, were saved through water [the flood]. There is also an antitype which now saves us—baptism" (1 Peter 3:20-21). Thus, Ananias said to Saul of Tarsus, "And now why are you waiting? Arise and be baptized, and wash away your sins, calling on the name of the Lord" (Acts 22:16). Baptism is the washing away and forgiveness of our sins.

"preparing them to be a temple of Your Holy Spirit". Baptism is preparing a person to be a temple for the Holy Spirit to dwell in them, "Do you not know that you are the temple of God and that the Spirit of God dwells in you? If anyone defiles the temple of God, God will destroy him. For the temple of God is holy, which temple you are" (1 Corinthians 3:16-17). "Or do you not know that your body is the temple of the Holy Spirit who is in you, whom you have from God, and you are not your own?" (1 Corinthians 6:19). It is after baptism that we receive the grace of adoption by God the Father, which prepares us for the dwelling of the Spirit within us. "Because you are sons, God has sent forth the Spirit of His Son into your hearts, crying out, "Abba, Father!" (Galatians 4:6).

May we preserve this great grace bestowed upon us through baptism and chrismation, making us a temple for the living God and a dwelling place for the Holy Spirit, holy members in the body of our Lord Jesus Christ.

CHAPTER 10

Covering Prayer

After reading the Gospel during the liturgy and following the sermon in which the priest (or whoever is designated) explains the passages of the readings used, the serving priest (conducting the divine liturgy on this day) stands before the "icon bearer" called "the veil," bowing his head to the east as a sign of submission and humility before God. He offers a deep prayer filled with the meanings of repentance and seeks divine assistance to complete the service of the liturgy before entering the sanctuary to celebrate the liturgy of the faithful, as if the priest is seeking God's permission to enter the sanctuary and pray.

Consider and contemplate, dear reader, how many times our priest humbly stands before God, seeking permission to carry out the service! The Holy Church teaches us the sacrament of humility and submission before God.

"As for me, I will come into Your house in the multitude of Your mercy; In fear of You, I will worship toward Your holy temple" (Psalm 5:7). "And the tax collector, standing afar off, would not so much as raise his eyes to heaven, but beat his breast, saying, 'God, be merciful to me, a sinner!'" (Luke 18:13).

Ibn Saba says: "The priest bows his head and recites a secret prayer outside the sanctuary before entering the temple, standing with bowed head as a sign of submission."[1]

---

[1] Youhanna bn Zakariya aka. Ibn Saba 13th century theologian. Author of the book Spritual gem in the Church (Arabic text). Quote found in said book page 213.

This is My Body

There are several prayers for the veil, and the priest chooses one to pray, depending on the liturgy he is about to celebrate: Basilian, Gregorian, or Cyrillian.

Now, let us reflect on the words of one of these prayers, composed by Saint James the Apostle, and prayed before the Basilian liturgy:

"O God, who in Your ineffable love toward mankind sent Your only-begotten Son into the world that He might return the lost sheep to You." Here, it is clear that the prayer is directed to the Father, and the lost sheep refers to Adam, for whom the Shepherd (the only begotten Son) left the angels (ninety-nine righteous ones who do not need repentance) and came to seek Adam, bringing him back to the heavenly fold. The priest mentions this to say, "Even if I am a lost human, You seek the lost, reject me not and accept me in Your service and the service of Your altar."

"We ask You, O our Master, turn us not back" … That is, do not reject my service before You because of my sins and weaknesses. "when we put our hands on this awesome and bloodless sacrifice." The Eucharistic sacrifice is called "bloodless" because it is a royal rite (bead and wine) and not Aaronic (goats, calves and sheep). Rather, just like Jesus says, the bread and wine are transformed into the true body and blood of Jesus Christ the Son of God:

"Take, eat; this is My body" (Matthew 26:26)

"For this is My blood of the new covenant, which is shed for many for the remission of sins." (Matthew 26:28)

"But we are all like an unclean thing, And all our righteousnesses are like filthy rags; We all fade as a leaf, And our iniquities, like the wind, Have taken us away" (Isaiah 64:6)".

We rely on mercy because, in terms of our righteousness, we know that we have not done good on earth. Instead, we rely on the righteousness of Christ.

"For in You, we do not trust in our righteousness but in Your mercy, by which You have given life to our race." "In those days Judah will be saved, And Jerusalem will dwell safely. And this is the name by which she will be called" (Jeremiah 33:16).

"O my God, incline Your ear and hear; open Your eyes and see our desolations, and the city which is called by Your name; for we do not present our supplications before You because of our righteous deeds, but because of Your great mercies" (Daniel 9: 18).

"Remember me, O my God, concerning this also, and spare me according to the greatness of Your mercy!" (Nehemiah 13:22).

"But I have trusted in Your mercy; My heart shall rejoice in Your salvation." (Psalm 13:5).

Do not allow, O my God, that this sacred sacrament, which You have established in the Church for our salvation, becomes a cause of judgement for us. For partaking of the Eucharist unworthily incurs judgement.

"Therefore whoever eats this bread or drinks this cup of the Lord in an unworthy manner will be guilty of the body and blood of the Lord" (1 Corinthians 11:27).

"For he who eats and drinks in an unworthy manner eats and drinks judgment to himself, not discerning the Lord's body" (1 Corinthians 11:29).

"But unto the wiping out of our sins, and the forgiveness of our negligence" (Prayer of the veil)

Amen, O my good God, make all Your people - and I am among them - worthy to partake of the eucharist worthily, to obtain forgiveness, eternal life, and everlasting salvation.

"And glory and honor to Your holy name, O Father, Son, and Holy Spirit." (St. Basil's liturgy)

It is communion that brings salvation to the people, and glorifies and honours the Holy name of God.

"The hour has come that the Son of Man should be glorified" (John 12:23).

"Now the Son of Man is glorified, and God is glorified in Him. If God is glorified in Him, God will also glorify Him in Himself, and glorify Him immediately" (John 13:31-32).

The greatest thing that glorifies God in His holy Church is the salvation of His people. This salvation cannot be without partaking of the body and blood of the Lord, according to His divine saying: "Most assuredly, I say to you, unless you eat the flesh of the Son of Man and drink His blood, you have no life in you. Whoever eats My flesh and drinks My blood has eternal life, and I will raise him up at the last day" (John 6:53-54).

CHAPTER

11

Prayer of Reconciliation

The Liturgy of the Faithful begins with the Prayer of Reconciliation, and by reconciliation here, we mean the meaning conveyed in Syrian fraction: "Uniting and reconciling the heavenly with the earthly, the people with the peoples, and the soul with the body."

Reconciliation and peace here are tri-direcetional: reconciling with heaven, with people, and with oneself. A person who does not know how to reconcile with oneself cannot reconcile with others or with God, who "has given us the ministry of reconciliation " (2 Corinthians 5:18). "We also rejoice in God through our Lord Jesus Christ, through whom we have now received the reconciliation" (Romans 5:11). Moreover, the one who "does not love his brother whom he has seen, how can he love God whom he has not seen? And this commandment we have from Him: that he who loves God must love his brother also." (1 John 4:20-21).

The Prayer of Reconciliation is always placed at the beginning in compliance with the command of the Lord Jesus: "Therefore if you bring your gift to the altar, and there remember that your brother has something against you, leave your gift there before the altar, and go your way. First be reconciled to your brother, and then come and offer your gift." (Matthew 5:23:24).

The sign of this reconciliation is the holy kiss. "Greet one another with a holy kiss" (1 Corinthians 16:20).

The prayers of reconciliation focus on the story of human salvation, through which our Lord reconciled us:

"For if when we were enemies we were reconciled to God through the death of His Son, much more, having been reconciled, we shall be saved by His life" (Romans 5:10).

"That is, that God was in Christ reconciling the world to Himself, not imputing their trespasses to them, and has committed to us the word of reconciliation" (2 Corinthians 5:19).

"Now then, we are ambassadors for Christ, as though God were pleading through us: we implore you on Christ's behalf, be reconciled to God" (2 Corinthians 5:20).

In the Prayer of Reconciliation, the priest approaches the altar and prays with bare hands, like Adam who became naked in Paradise after sin. After reconciliation, he puts on two altar cloths on his hands because he has clothed himself with the precious salvation of our Lord Jesus Christ.

Reflections on the Basilian Prayer of Reconciliation:

In the Basilian Prayer of Reconciliation, we pray: "O God, the Great the Eternal (without beginning or end), who formed (created or built) man in incorruption (immortality- God created us to live forever and this is an extra blessing that was conditional on man's preservation of God's image. However, if this image is lost or distorted, man becomes in danger of returning to death); and death, which entered into the world through the envy of the devil (death entered because of Satan's envy towards humans), You have destroyed (through the cross "having wiped out the handwriting of requirements that was against us, which was contrary to us. And He has taken it out of the way, having nailed it to the cross" (Colossians 2:14)) by Your life giving manifestation of Your only-begotten Son, our Lord, God, and saviour Jesus Christ". The appearance of the Lord Christ on earth, was a life giving appearance because:

"In Him was life, and the life was the light of men." (John 1:4).

"Jesus said to her, "I am the resurrection and the life. He who believes in Me, though he may die, he shall live" (John 11:25).

"Most assuredly, I say to you, he who hears My word and believes in Him who sent Me has everlasting life, and shall not come into judgment, but has passed from death into life." (John 5:24).

"You filled the Earth with Your heavenly peace, this which the host of angels glorify you saying "Glory to God in the highest, peace on earth and good will toward men". This is the hymn that the angels praised at the birth of the Lord Jesus Christ, expressing the glory of God manifested in the salvation of humanity through incarnation and the cross, and also the peace of God that has come to the earth.

In the Prayer of Reconciliation, the priest takes the triangular cloth placed above the prospherin, which indicates the seal of the tomb after the burial of the Savior, and lifts it. The lifting of this cloth, signifies the removal of the seals from the tomb, and thus, the lifting of the prospherin announces the resurrection, which occurs during the holy kiss. During this, the deacon stands opposite the priest, holding the cross.

The priest continues, "With your goodness O God, fill our hearts with your peace ("and the peace of God, which surpasses all understanding, will guard your hearts and minds through Christ Jesus" (Philippians 4:7). Cleanse us from all blemish, all guile all hypocrisy, all craftiness and the remembrance of vice bearing death (the sins and pitfalls hinder the peace between people and between them and God). Make us worthy, O our Master to greet one another with a holy kiss (which is the aim of the prayer of reconciliation) so that, without casting us into condemnation ("Therefore whoever eats this bread or drinks this cup of the Lord in an unworthy manner will be guilty of the body and blood of the Lord" (1 Corinthians 11:27) and "For he who eats and drinks in an unworthy manner eats and drinks judgment to himself, not discerning the Lord's body" (1 Corinthians 11:29)), we may partake of Your immortal and heavenly gift (the Body and the Blood)".

The Anaphora- Meet and right

When then the priest says "Let us give thanks to the Lord" in the beginning of the Anaphora, the congregation responds "meet and right". This means that it is a duty and fitting to thank the Lord. This is the same phrase used by the priest in the Liturgy of St. Cyril: "For truly it is fitting and right, and holy and becoming, and profitable to our souls, bodies, and spirits…to praise You, hymn You, bless You, serve You, worship You, thank You, glorify You. And confess to You….".

St. Augustine of the fourth century said, "Let us thank Him, for if He did not bestow His grace upon us, our hearts would remain attached to the earth. You testify to this and say that it is meet and right that we thank the One who lifted our hearts to where our Head is."

From here, in the liturgy, until the coming of the Holy Spirit, it is called the "Great Thanksgiving Prayer." It includes thanking God for creation, then for the incarnation of the only Son and His redeeming sufferings, and then the institution narrative or what the Lord Christ did in establishing the sacrament on Covenant Thursday.

Meet and right:

The priest prays, saying, "Meet and right" three times, "O You THE BEING, Master, Lord, God of Truth, being before the ages and reigning forever; who dwells in the highest and looks upon the lowly; who has created the heaven, the earth , the sea, and all that is therein". Here, the priest describes the person of our great God, explaining what we know about Him, and thanking Him for what He has done for us in terms of His creation from nothing.

"God is good- or rather, of all goodness He is Fountainhead, and it is impossible for one who is good to be mean or grudging about anything. Grudging existence to none therefore, He made all things out of nothing through His own Word, our Lord Jesus Christ; and of all these His earthly creatures He reserved especial mercy for the race of men. Upon them, therefore, upon men who, as animals, were essentially impermanent, He bestowed a grace which other creatures lacked- namely, the impress of His own Image, a share in the reasonable being of the very Word Himself, so that, reflecting Him and themselves becoming reasonable and expressing the Mind of God even as He does, though in limited degree, they might continue forever in the blessed and only true life of the saints in paradise" (On the Incarnation of the Word by St. Athanasius the Apostolic).

The priest continues, "the Father of our Lord, God, and Saviour Jesus Christ, by whom You have created all things, visible and invisible; who is seated upon the throne of His glory and who is worshiped by all the holy powers". And interspersed are two responses from the deacons: "you who are seated stand", and "look to the east".

The first response means, "Attention of the mind and spirit as the people stand before the same call". The second response means, "Attention to the altar and the holy sacrifice on it, as the people are also naturally facing eastward throughout the prayer". Therefore, we must stand at all times with a prepared heart, with our hearts connected to the altar without distraction.

Before the Cherubic hymn, the deacon calls, "Let us attend," as if urging us to listen to the voices of the cherubim praising, so that we can join in their holy praise. And with the same words: "Holy, holy, holy."

The Cherubic hymn:

"Holy, holy, holy Lord of Sabaoth. Heaven and earth are full of Your holy glory". We learned this hymn from the vision of Isaiah: "I saw the Lord sitting on a throne, high and lifted up, and the train of His robe filled the temple. Above it stood seraphim; each one had six wings: with two he covered his face, with two he covered his feet, and with two he flew. And one cried to another and said: "Holy, holy, holy is the Lord of hosts; The whole earth is full of His glory!"" (Isaiah 6:1-3).

And we precede this hymn with a description of this heavenly scene.

In the Basilian Liturgy, we pray, saying: "Before whom stand the angels, the archangels, the principalities, the authorities, the thrones, the dominions, and the powers. You are He around who stand the cherubim full of eyes, and the seraphim with six wings, praising continuously, without ceasing saying…."

In the Gregorian Liturgy, this description is enhanced with superlative spiritual beauty, as it says: "who has established the rising of the choir of the incorporeal (the angels) among men, who has given to the earthly (humans) the praising of the seraphim, receive from us also our voices, together with the invisible (the angels). Count us with the heavenly hosts. Let us also say with them (the angels)… and proclaim that which they send up with unceasing voices and unfailing lips, and praise Your greatness… You are He around who stand the cherubim and the seraphim, six wings to the one and six wings to the other, with two they cover their faces and with two they cover their feet, and with two they fly. And one cries to another. They send up the hymn of victory and salvation which is ours, with a voice full of glory. They praise, they sing, they proclaim, they cry out saying…"

In the Cyril Liturgy, he elaborates on this heavenly scene: "You are He before who stand thousands of thousands and ten thousand times ten thousand of holy angels and archangels serving You. You are He before who stand Your two most honoured living creatures, with their six wings and many eyes, the seraphim and the cherubim. With two wings they cover their faces on account of Your divinity that cannot be beheld or comprehended, and with two they cover their feet and with the other two they fly. For at all times, all hallow You. But with all who hallow You receive from us- we, too- our hallowing, O Lord, as we praise You with them, saying…"

After the people finish chanting the Cherubic hymn, the priest prays a prayer that begins in all the liturgies with the phrase: "Holy, Holy, Holy," as if the liturgy explains the synergy and partnership between the priest, the people, and the deacon. After "Holy," the priest recounts the story of creation, the fall, the incarnation, redemption, and the second coming. He says, "Who formed us, created us, and placed us in the paradise of joy" … that is, the original state that the Lord intended for us.

"When we disobeyed Your command by the deceit of the serpent, we fell from eternal life and were exiled from the paradise of joy,"… a situation we brought upon ourselves, a situation we repeat daily.

God places us in very good, enjoyable, and joyful circumstances, then we bring upon ourselves sorrow, destruction, and loss because we choose sin willingly, despite our knowledge of its harm and danger. Nevertheless, "You have not abandoned us to the end, but have always visited us to Your holy prophets." God never abandons us; He always commits to caring, following up, warning, encouraging, and admonishing us, using all means for our salvation through fathers, teachers, servants, and educators.

"In the last days, You manifested Yourself to us, who were sitting in darkness and the shadow of death". "Last days here" refers to the fullness of time, the time of the incarnation. However, we can also understand this phrase spiritually that God will not leave us in our perdition and negligence until the end of our lives. He will pursue us with attempts and warnings until the last breath.

Lord Jesus, I thank You for Your hope in me and for the repeated opportunities You give me to repent. Let me benefit from these divine invocations, do not deliver me to a rejected mind, and allow me to return to You before the grave swallows me. O God, visit me with Your abundant mercies, even if it's in the last days, and consider me like the repentant thief. O God, do not take me in heedlessness or in wasted time. Instead, allow me to be taken on a day of longing, prayer, altar and liturgy. Amen.

"You appeared to us… through You only-begotten Son, our Lord, God and Saviour Jesus Christ"… for we saw the Father through His Son, our Lord Jesus Christ.

"And he who sees Me sees Him who sent Me" (John 12:45).

"He who has seen Me has seen the Father" (John 14:9).

"who, of the Holy Spirit and of the holy Virgin Mary, was incarnate and became man". The Lord Jesus was incarnate of St Mary through the Holy Spirit.

"And the angel answered and said to her, "The Holy Spirit will come upon you, and the power of the Highest will overshadow you; therefore, also, that Holy One who is to be born will be called the Son of God." (Luke 1:35).

"and taught us the ways of salvation"… Our Lord Jesus is the only way to salvation. "Nor is there salvation in any other, for there is no other name under heaven given among men by which we must be saved." (Acts 4:12). But this precious salvation is obtained in many ways. Therefore, the liturgy uses the plural form (ways) and not (way). These ways are baptism, the indwelling of the Holy Spirit, repentance, the Eucharist, and prayer. There are also other ways to salvation, such as monasticism, marriage, service, and witnessing. Some people are saved through toil, hardships, diseases, and problems, and all of these can be a means of salvation for them. God alone knows the path of salvation for each one of us. Let us entrust our lives to Him, that He may direct them as he sees befitting and according to His divine wisdom, and let everything be according to His will.

A brother was called to the priestly ministry and was afraid because he highly valued its seriousness of the responsibility of the salvation of each person in the congregation. So, he went to his spiritual father for guidance. He said to him, "Pray and say, 'O Lord, if the call to the priesthood, with all its hardships and responsibilities, is the path to my salvation, let it be according to Your will. But if it leads to my destruction, I beg You to clearly divert me in Your way.'"

"He granted us the birth from on high through water and Spirit." The grace of baptism is one of the greatest blessings that God has bestowed on His holy Church. Through it, we become children of God, as it is written, "behold what manner of love the Father has bestowed on us, that we should be called children of God!" (1 John 3:1). It is an extraordinary love, "Thanks be to God for His indescribable gift!" (2 Corinthians 9:15).

"He made us unto Himself and assembled people"… the attribute of this people is that they are assembled continuously, without interruption. We can join this assembly through the liturgy which we pray together in all the churches, using the same words, tunes, readings and season (feast or fast). Likewise we are always in an assembled state because of the one shared faith, the one baptism, and of course, One God… "one Lord, one faith, one baptism" (Ephesians 4:5)

Blessed is he who always preserves his assembly with the church, and does not separate from it, neither deviating from the faith nor practice.

"and sanctified us by Your Holy Sprit"… holiness and purity is not the fruit of effort and human competence, rather it is the grace of the Holy Spirit that dwells in us. Let us preserve this grace, and whoever receives this grace should not boast as though he obtained it with his own power or piety.

"For who makes you differ from another? And what do you have that you did not receive? Now if you did indeed receive it, why do you boast as if you had not received it?" (1 Corinthians 4:7)

"He loved His own who were in the world"…"having loved His own who were in the world, He loved them to the end" (John 13:1). And the proof of this divine love is the precious salvation through the cross, "For God so loved the world that He gave His only begotten Son, that whoever believes in Him should not perish but have everlasting life." (John 3:16). For "greater love has no one than this, than to lay down one's life for his friends" (John 15:13).

"gave Himself up unto death, which reined over us"… truly O God, death reigned over us and sin took control over the old man. I have no salvation except through Your Son my holy Master.

"death… whereby we were bound and sold on account of our sin"… death bound our bodies since the fall of Adam, and we had no salvation except through the incarnation of the Only Begotten Son, so that He defeats death by His death, and raises us from its rule with His resurrection.

"He descended into Hades through the Cross"… The Lord descended into Hades after He died on the Cross to free the captives, then ascended with them from Hades to Paradise. "Now this, "He ascended"—what does it mean but that He also first descended into the lower parts of the earth?" (Ephesians 4:9). He freed the people from the bondage of the devil. "Therefore He says: "When He ascended on high, He led captivity captive, and gave gifts to men."" (Ephesians 4:8). It was a very joyous moment for the righteous souls who were captives in the darkness of Hades, when Christ our Lord came to free them from their prisons… "by whom also He went and preached to the spirits in prison" (1 Peter 3:19).

"He rose from the dead on the third day. He ascended into the heavens and sat at Your right hand, O Father". The story of salvation does not stop at crucifixion and death, rather He who was crucified for our sake, rose also for our sake. "who was delivered up because of our offenses, and was raised because of our justification" (Romans 4:25). He also ascended to Heaven for our sake, "where the forerunner has entered for us, even Jesus" (Hebrews 6:20). And sat at the right hand of the Father, also for our sake that He may intercede for us with His pure blood, a propitiatory intercession. "who is even at the right hand of God, who also makes intercession for us" (Romans 8:34).

"He appointed a day for recompense, on which He will appear to judge the world in righteousness, and give each one according to his deeds"… "because He has appointed a day on which He will judge the world in righteousness by the Man whom He has ordained. He has given assurance of this to all by raising Him from the dead." (Acts 17:31). Let us all be made aware that judgement will be based on deeds and not just faith. Lest anyone rely on his faith, thinking that God will favour Him because of his faith because:

"In truth I perceive that God shows no partiality" (Acts 10:34).

"who "will render to each one according to his deeds"" (Romans 2:6).

"all the churches shall know that I am He who searches the minds and hearts. And I will give to each one of you according to your works" (Revelations 2:23).

"And I saw the dead, small and great, standing before God, and books were opened. And another book was opened, which is the Book of Life. And the dead were judged according to their works, by the things which were written in the books. The sea gave up the dead who were in it, and Death and Hades delivered up the dead who were in them. And they were judged, each one according to his works." (Revelations 20:12-13). Therefore we cry out saying, "According to Your mercy O Lord, and not according to our sins".

Yes, O Lord, let Your mercy be the measuring standard and not our sins, "If You, Lord, should mark iniquities, O Lord, who could stand?" (Psalm 130:3). And by my works, I have no salvation. Grant me salvation by Your mercy, O Lord of all, for there is no servant without sin and no master without forgiveness.

Interchange of altar cloths

The priest signs the people with the altar cloth that was covering the paten when he turns to the west and says "The Lord be with you all" at the beginning of the Anaphora. Likewise, when he says "Agios", he signs the people with the altar cloth that was covering the chalice.

There is a beautiful contemplation regarding this interchange of altar cloths. In the beginning, the priest covers his right hand with the altar cloth that was covering the paten and signs the people with it. He covers his left hand with the altar cloth that was on top of the prospherin, this cloth which symbolises the seal on the tomb of our Saviour, to represent the sins of the congregation which became a barrier between God and people. This is also why the priest covers his eye with it in the second part of the prayer of reconciliation. After the lifting of the prospherin and the annunciation of reconciliation between God and man, he places the altar cloth that was on top of the prospherin on his left hand because the right symbolises righteousness. Therefore, his right hand is covered by the righteousness of Christ, that is, with the altar cloth that was covering the holy sacrifice (paten), and his left hand is covered with the altar cloth that symbolises our sins that obscure from us God's face.

Before "Agios" the priest interchanges the altar cloths, placing the altar cloth that was on his left hand on the chalice, that is to say, our sins have been cast upon the chalice of the Blood of Christ because He is "The Lamb of God who takes away the sin of the world!" (John 1:29).

As for the cloth on his right hand, he places it on his left hand, as if Christ has lifted our sins from us, covered us with the righteousness of His body, and transferred us from the left to the right.

Then the cloth that was on the chalice is used to sign the congregation with the sign of the cross saying "Agios, Agios" because we draw all holiness from the blood of the Lord Christ. Then he covers his right hand with it, so we become saints, covered with the blood of Christ.

Meanwhile, while all this is happening, another priest goes around the altar, offering incense, like the heavenly scene: "Then another angel, having a golden censer, came and stood at the altar. He was given much incense, that he should offer it with the prayers of all the saints upon the golden altar which was before the throne. And the smoke of the incense, with the prayers of the saints, ascended before God from the angel's hand" (Revelations 8:3-4).

The prayers following "Agios" narrate the history of salvation from creation to the second coming, passing through the fall, incarnation, and redemption, as explained earlier.

Institution Narrative

The words of institution are the words spoken by our Lord on the bread and wine to consecrate them into His pure Body and Blood.

In the liturgy, we repeat the same words as if they were from the mouth of Christ Himself, believing in His holy presence to sanctify the offerings. "O You who did bless at that time, now also bless… O You who did sanctify at that time, now also sanctify… He who did break at that time, now also break… He who gave… at that time, now also give to us…"

Prayer of Reconciliation

In the Coptic liturgy, the words of consecration are called "signs" and begin with the phrase: "He has instituted for us this great Mystery of godliness" ending with the response: "Your death, O Lord, we proclaim." These words are taken directly from the Holy Scriptures:

"For I received from the Lord that which I also delivered to you: that the Lord Jesus on the same night in which He was betrayed took bread; and when He had given thanks, He broke it and said, "Take, eat; this is My body which is broken for you; do this in remembrance of Me." In the same manner He also took the cup after supper, saying, "This cup is the new covenant in My blood. This do, as often as you drink it, in remembrance of Me." For as often as you eat this bread and drink this cup, you proclaim the Lord's death till He comes" (1 Corinthians 11:23-26).

"And as they were eating, Jesus took bread, blessed and broke it, and gave it to the disciples and said, "Take, eat; this is My body." Then He took the cup, and gave thanks, and gave it to them, saying, "Drink from it, all of you. For this is My blood of the new covenant, which is shed for many for the remission of sins" (Matthew 26:26-28).

The priest censes his hand over the censer three times, to purify them and to confess the partnership of the Holy Trinity in the salvation of the human race, before taking the offering with both hands. He catches some of the rising incense from the censer to proclaim that when Christ offered himself as an acceptable sacrifice on the Cross, His Good father smelled him as a pleasing aroma. The deacons light candles around the altar, symbolizing the act of enlightenment that the sacrifice of Christ brings to us.

All of this is done while the priest says, "He instituted for us this great Mystery of godliness".

When the priest says, "He took bread..." he takes the offering in his hands, lifts the cloth underneath it on the pattern, kisses it, wipes it over his eyes, then raises his gaze upward, saying, "He looked up".

When he says, "He broke it," he begins to break the offering without separating its parts, keeping the back intact, signifying the sufferings of Christ and the tearing of His body without breaking His bones, as prophesied, "nor shall you break one of its bones" (Exodus 12:46).

When he begins the consecration of the cup, he places his finger on the rim of the chalice, tracing it clockwise and then counterclockwise, indicating that this cup at this time is the very cup that Christ used at that time, a temporal and eternal cup.

St Ephrem the Syrian says, "He called the bread His living Body, and did Himself fill it with Himself and the Spirit.... Take, eat, entertaining no doubt of faith, because this is My Body, and whoever eats it in belief eats in it Fire and Spirit. Eat of it all of you, eat in it the Holy Spirit, for it is my body in truth".

According to the patristic fathers, we partake of the real body of Christ in the form of bread and His precious blood in the form of wine. The presence of Christ in the sacraments is not a material or spiritual presence but a sacramental and real presence simultaneously.

Orthodox theology has affirmed the teaching of the fathers, emphasizing the real presence of Christ in the Eucharist and the transformation of bread and wine into the body and blood of Christ, without attempting to explain this transformation in the language of philosophy.

The bread and wine, through the words of consecration and the invocation of the Holy Spirit, become the body and holy blood of Christ. This is the precise expression in the text of the Coptic liturgical prayers. We cannot limit the consecration of the elements of the sacrifice in the Divine Liturgy to a discrete, stand-alone moment or utterance.

The Invocation

Saint Irenaeus of the second century AD says, "The bread... when it receives the invocation of God, is no longer common bread, but the Eucharist"

The term "invocation" means that the priest prays the prayer of the coming of the Holy Spirit, imploring Him to come and dwell on the offerings placed, changing them into the Holy Body and Blood of the Lord. While the priest and the entire congregation are prostrated, he says, "we ask You, O Lord our God- we Your sinful and unworthy servants worship You by the pleasure of Your goodness- that Your Holy Spirit may descend upon us and upon these gifts set forth, and purify them, change them, and manifest them as a sanctification of Your saints"

Then the priest makes three crosses quickly over the offering (before pronouncing the word "body") while saying, "This bread He makes into His holy body."

The people prostrate and say, "I believe. Amen."

The priest extends his hands and bows, saying inaudibly, "Our Lord, God and Saviour Jesus Christ, given for the remission of sins and eternal life to those who partake of Him."

He repeats the same with the chalice, making three crosses quickly, saying, "And this cup also, the precious blood of His new covenant". He continues as before, saying inaudibly, "Our Lord, God, and Saviour Jesus Christ, given for the remission of sins and eternal life to those who partake of it".

The congregation rises from prostration, joyfully and spiritually glorifying, saying, "Amen. Lord, have mercy. Lord, have mercy. Lord, have mercy".

The priest's supplication for the invocation of the Holy Spirit is closely akin to the prayers in the Bible where we seek the coming of the Holy Spirit.

"Do not cast me away from Your presence, and do not take Your Holy Spirit from me" (Psalm 51:11).

"You send forth Your Spirit, they are created; and You renew the face of the earth."" (Psalm 104:30).

"and sent your Holy Spirit from on high" (Wisdom 9:17).

Here, the Holy Spirit has descended upon the offerings, sanctified them, and transformed them into the true body and precious blood of the Lord. He did this own will for the forgiveness of our sins, such that we may attain forgiveness and benefiting from the Cross of Christ, by partaking in this great sacrament by eating from it according to the saying of our Good Lord:

"Whoever eats My flesh and drinks My blood has eternal life, and I will raise him up at the last day" (John 6:54).

"He who eats My flesh and drinks My blood abides in Me, and I in him" (John 6:56).

"As the living Father sent Me, and I live because of the Father, so he who feeds on Me will live because of Me" (John 6:57).

"This is the bread which came down from heaven—not as your fathers ate the manna, and are dead. He who eats this bread will live forever" (John 6:58).

My Lord Jesus, allow me to partake of this heavenly bread and drink from your precious Blood without discontinuity. Grant me, with all Your people, not to be deprived of this heavenly and holy banquet every day.

O Spirit of the Holy God, as you descend upon a simple offering, by your divine act, you transform it into the most upright and precious thing in existence—the pure Body of the Lord, the Savior, and the life-giver for all who unite with Him through this holy morsel.

O God, please dwell within me, transform me from my insignificance, depravity and uselessness, to a vessel suitable to serve of your Holy name, and an edification to the Church. For you have always chosen the weak and the uneducated to perform great works through them.

"But we have this treasure in earthen vessels, that the excellence of the power may be of God and not of us" (2 Corinthians 4:7).

"But God has chosen the foolish things of the world to put to shame the wise, and God has chosen the weak things of the world to put to shame the things which are mighty; and the base things of the world and the things which are despised God has chosen, and the things which are not, to bring to nothing the things that are that no flesh should glory in His presence" (1 Corinthians 1:27-28).

"Listen, my beloved brethren: Has God not chosen the poor of this world to be rich in faith and heirs of the kingdom which He promised to those who love Him?" (James 2:5).

Post Commemoration[1] of the saints and Diptych[2]

After the diptych, the priest prays, saying, "That as in this, so also in all things, Your great and holy name may be glorified, blessed, and exalted in everything honoured and blessed with Jesus Christ, Your beloved Son, and the Holy Spirit." The sacrament of the Eucharist is the sacrament by which the great and holy name is glorified, blessed, and exalted in everything. This great and blessed name is also glorified, blessed and exalted in everything in the creation, care, and salvation. This is the intended meaning of this sacred phrase found in all the liturgies of our Coptic Church.

It is preceded by the response of the congregation, "As it was, and shall be, its is from generation to generation… Amen". In ancient times, this response was said after the priest's prayer, not before it. Thus, its meaning becomes clearer, saying, "As it was in every generation, may Your holy and great name be glorified and blessed and exalted in everything, as it is now and forever."

Then the father priest raises his hands upwards and thanks God, the commander of all, saying, "for He has made us worthy now to stand in this holy place (the altar which is Heaven), to lift up our hands, and to serve His holy name." Our presence in the church and our practice of prayer are great blessings that we do not deserve, so we thank our good God who has bestowed upon us this sacred gift.

"Let us also ask Him to make us worthy of the communion and partaking of His divine and immortal mysteries". He who has given us the right and worthiness to stand in the altar and heaven, we implore Him to grant us the qualification and worthiness to partake

1 This is explained in the chapter "saints in the holy liturgy".
2 This is explained in the chapter "litanies: litany of the departed".

of the holy mysteries.

The Fraction

The father priest holds the holy body in his hand and begins to divide it while praying prayers that change according to the occasion celebrated by the church. The prayer is somewhat sad because the division symbolizes the salvific sufferings of Christ.

The people respond after each segment with the response: "Kyrie Eleyson" (Lord, have mercy) three times, seeking mercy and forgiveness through the Blood shed on the cross, of the only Son, which we are about to drink shortly.

The confession

After the prayers said by the father priest inaudibly after the fraction… the people lift their heads because they have received forgiveness through repentance, prayer, and the absolution prayed by the priest

The priest takes the "Ispatikon" (the middle part of the Eucharist) and raises it high, dipping it into the cup of the holy blood. With it, he makes the sign of the cross over the Body, saying: "The holies (meaning the Body and Blood) for the holies (the believing congregation present in the liturgy, now made pure and holy by the action of the Holy Spirit and prayers)."

Then he glorifies God, saying: "Blessed by the Lord Jesus Christ, the Son of God; the sanctification is by the Holy Spirit. Amen".

St Cyril of Jerusalem says, "Holy are the gifts presented, having received the visitation of the Holy Ghost; holy are you also, having been deemed worthy of the Holy Ghost; the holy things therefore correspond to the holy persons".[3]

He also says in his 17th sermon in his explanation of the letter to the Hebrews, "the church cries out with this phrase so that any human who is not holy should not approach…the Church does not loudly proclaim that only he who is without sin should approach, however,

3 Catechetical Lecture 23

he who has the Holy Spirit and holds fast to good deeds shall come forward". "He declares that with respect to holiness, there is but one Holy, the Father, the Son and the Holy Spirit"

The congregation responds with this Trinitarian glorification, "One is the Holy Father (only one is holy who is the Father), one is the Holy Son, One is the Holy Spirit (same meaning)".

Then the priest declares the faith of the Church regarding the truth of this sacrament, so he holds a segment of the Body in his hands and says three variations of, "The Holy Body and the precious, true Blood of Jesus Christ, the Son of Our God. Amen". Then he prays the confession, "this is the life-giving Flesh that Your only-begotten Son, our Lord, God, and Saviour Jesus Christ, took holy Virgin Mary. He made It one with His divinity from the first moment of the divine incarnation without mingling, without confusion, and without alteration. He became one nature, one person, one hypostasis, God the incarnated logos without parting for a single moment, nor a twinkling of an eye".

The Christ confessed before Pontius Pilate (that he is the true Son of God), as our teacher St Paul wrote, "I urge you in the sight of God who gives life to all things, and before Christ Jesus who witnessed the good confession before Pontius Pilate" (1 Timothy 6:13).

It is likewise written in the narrative of the Lord Christ's crucifixion:

"Now Jesus stood before the governor. And the governor asked Him, saying, "Are You the King of the Jews?" Jesus said to him, "It is as you say."" (Matthew 27:11).

"Pilate therefore said to Him, "Are You a king then?" Jesus answered, "You say rightly that I am a king. For this cause I was born, and for this cause I have come into the world, that I should bear witness to the truth. Everyone who is of the truth hears My voice" (John 18:37).

Then the priest declares that the Lord Christ gave Himself up for us on the cross, of His own will.

"Jesus therefore, knowing all things that would come upon Him, went forward and said to them, "Whom are you seeking?"" (John 18:4).

"No one takes it from Me, but I lay it down of Myself. I have power to lay it down, and I have power to take it again. This command I have received from My Father" (John 6:51).

"Then Jesus said to them, "Most assuredly, I say to you, unless you eat the flesh of the Son of Man and drink His blood, you have no life in you. Whoever eats My flesh and drinks My blood has eternal life, and I will raise him up at the last day" (John 6:53-54).

"As the living Father sent Me, and I live because of the Father, so he who feeds on Me will live because of Me" (John 6:57).

My Lord Jesus, O secret of my life, my perpetuity and eternity… To you is my life, because it is Yours from the beginning. For You are my creator, Saviour and life-giver.

During the partaking of the holy Body and Blood of the Lord, we chant praises and hymns that befit this heavenly joy and this inexpressible gift.

Saint Clement the Alexandrian says: "Praise Him with the sound of the trumpet; for with the sound of the trumpet, He will call the sleepers to resurrection. Praise Him with the harp; the tongue that is the harp of the Lord. Praise Him with the lute; and the mouth when moved by the Holy Spirit is like the lute. Praise Him with timbrel and dance; it refers to the church contemplating the resurrection from the dead through the striking of the dead skin. Praise Him with stringed instruments and organs; the organ is the body, and its nerves are the strings, signed by our human voices when we are in harmony with the Holy Spirit. Praise Him with pleasant sounding cymbals; refers to the lips of the mouth when praise falls upon them. Every that has breath praise the name of the Lord; here, all humanity is called to praise, for He cares for every breathing creature. Truly man is an instrument of peace. However, because of races, each race uses an instrument of these to declare war. There remains only one machine for peace, and it is "the word" alone. So, we do not use the trumpet or the harp or the drum or the horn used by those who specialise in wars and in their celebrations. Isn't the ten-stringed harp a sign of the word "Jesus" since the word "Jesus" begins in Greek with the letter (Iota), which represents the number 10.

CHAPTER 12

Agbeya

Arrangement of the Canonical Hours during the Divine Liturgy: The Canonical Hours are a book of daily prayers arranged according to the hours, where we pray seven daytime prayers and three nighttime prayers, following the teachings of the Holy Scriptures: "Seven times a day I praise You, Because of Your righteous judgments." (Psalm 119:164). These prayers are as follows:

1. Prime Prayer: prayed at 6:00 AM, commemorating the resurrection of the Lord Jesus Christ from the dead.

2. Terce Prayer: prayed at 9:00 AM, remembering the descent of the Holy Spirit upon our apostolic fathers on the fiftieth day; it also commemorates the trial of our righteous Savior.

3. Sext Prayer: prayed at 12:00 PM, commemorating the crucifixion of the Lord Jesus Christ.

4. None Prayer: prayed at 3:00 PM, commemorating the death of the Lord Jesus Christ.

5. Vespers Prayer: prayed at 5:00 PM, commemorating the descent of the body of the Lord Jesus Christ from the cross.

6. Compline Prayer: prayed at 6:00 PM, commemorating the burial of the Lord Jesus Christ.

7. The Veil Prayer: prayed by the monastic fathers at the end of the day as the veil of the night falls .

8. Midnight Prayers: at midnight, we pray three additional prayers, reflecting the three times that the Lord Jesus Christ prayed in the Garden of Gethsemane. In these prayers, we remember the second coming of Christ and prepare for the eternal life.

"At midnight I will rise to give thanks to You, Because of Your righteous judgments." (Psalm 119:62).

"My eyes are awake through the night watches, That I may meditate on Your word." (Psalm 119:148).

"Arise, cry out in the night, At the beginning of the watches; Pour out your heart like water before the face of the Lord. Lift your hands toward Him" (Lamentations 2:19).

These prayers are prayed daily, each individual in their room, as per the words of the Lord Jesus: "But you, when you pray, go into your room, and when you have shut your door, pray to your Father who is in the secret place; and your Father who sees in secret will reward you openly." (Matthew 6:6). We also pray them collectively in the church throughout the liturgical day.

Before the raising of the morning incense, we pray the Psalms of the Prime and the Morning Doxology. Before the presentation of the offerings, we pray the Psalms of the Canonical Hours according to the following schedule:

- During fasting periods, we pray (Terce, Sext, and None) since the liturgy may end late due to abstinent fasting.

- On non-fasting days (Feast Days), we pray (Terce and Sext only). This also applies to Saturdays, Sundays, annual feasts, and fixed feast days (even if they fall during fasting days).

- Before the raising of the evening incense, we pray the remaining Canonical Hour prayers. During fasting days, we pray (Vespers and Compline only), and on non-fasting days, we pray (None, Vespers, and Compline). Before the Midnight Praises, we pray the Midnight prayer, completing the liturgical day.

Special Exceptions:

1. During the Great Lent, excluding Saturdays and Sundays, and during the Nineveh Fast, we pray in the liturgy (Terce, Sext, None, Vespers, and Compline). We do not pray the raising of the evening incense because the liturgy ends late due to abstinent fasting.

2. On the Feast of the Pentecost, we specifically pray the Terce only, focusing on the event celebrated on this day, the descent of the Holy Spirit upon the disciples at 9:00 AM. In the evening of the same day, we pray the remaining hours (Sext, None, Vespers and Compline) before the Holy Prostration Praises.

3. On major feast days (Christmas, Epiphany, and Resurrection), we do not pray the Canonical Hours, as we celebrate the liturgy at an unusual time (midnight). Instead, we pray a set of Psalms that prophesy the event celebrated, known as the "Great Hos," before the Midnight Praises.

4. During the Holy Pascha, we do not use the Canonical Hours but replace them with the Paschal Prayers according to their order.

CHAPTER

13

Repentance

Repentance in Orthodox thought is a lifelong, continuous process—not a single decisive moment from which one moves on to another stage. It is the journey of life. Our teacher, the Apostle Paul, expressed this ongoing journey with the phrase "renewing of the mind": "And do not be conformed to this world, but be transformed by the renewing of your mind, that you may prove what is that good and acceptable and perfect will of God" (Romans 12:2).

The term used in the Church to signify the bowing down and repentance is "metanoia," representing not only our continuous prostration before God but also our perpetual turning back to Him. "Now God commands all men everywhere to repent, because He has appointed a day on which He will judge the world in righteousness" (Acts 17:30). He warns everyone against neglecting repentance, stating, "unless you repent, you will all likewise perish" (Luke 13:3). It is good for us to remember that Jesus Christ began His earthly ministry with a call to repentance: "From that time Jesus began to preach and to say, 'Repent, for the kingdom of heaven is at hand'" (Matthew 4:17).

The believer who does not consider himself in need of repentance removes himself from the sphere of Christ's work because, as He said, "Those who are well have no need of a physician, but those who are sick. I did not come to call the righteous, but sinners, to repentance" (Mark 2:17). The righteous and holy person always feels a sense of shortcoming in his service to Christ our God due to the magnitude of what Christ has done for us out of love. "So likewise you, when you have done all those things which you are commanded, say, 'We are unprofitable servants. We have done what was our duty to do'" (Luke 17:10). If the righteous person feels this way, how much more so the sinners who fall short! Indeed, "if the righteous one is scarcely saved, where will the ungodly and the sinner appear?" (1 Peter 4:18).

Therefore, repentance is a lifelong narrative, practiced every day until the last breath. There is no distinction in this between beginners and advanced, for we are all beginners when we look at Christ, discovering our weakness and unworthiness, just like our Father Abraham, who said, "Indeed now, I who am but dust and ashes have taken it upon myself to speak to the Lord" (Genesis 18:27). This is the same expression used by the wise Sirach about humanity: "He marshals the host of the height of heaven; but all human beings are dust and ashes." (Sirach 17:32).

Even the angels themselves diminish in the presence of the majesty of God: "If He puts no trust in His servants, if He charges His angels with error " (Job 4:18), how much more, then, the human being! Therefore, we are completely abased in the dust when we appear before the Lord in prayer, counting ourselves as the worst of sinners. This is the same as what our teacher, the Apostle Paul, said: "This is a faithful saying and worthy of all acceptance, that Christ Jesus came into the world to save sinners, of whom I am chief" (1 Timothy 1:15). Knowing that "the sacrifices of God are a broken spirit, a broken and a contrite heart—these, O God, You will not despise" (Psalm 51:17). We liken ourselves to the tax collector who was written about "And the tax collector, standing afar off, would not so much as raise his eyes to heaven, but beat his breast, saying, 'God, be merciful to me a sinner!' I tell you, this man went down to his house justified rather than the other; for everyone who exalts himself will be humbled, and he who humbles himself will be exalted." (Luke 18:13-14)

The Church, therefore, never ceases to ask for mercy throughout the Divine Liturgy: "Lord, have mercy", "Kyrie Eleyson", "According to Your mercy O Lord, and not according to our sins", the hymn of "Je nai nan", "Remember O Lord to have mercy on us all". The Liturgy

Repentance

is s a continuous plea, asking for mercy from the opening of the altar veil where the priest says, "Eleyson Eemas, Have mercy on us O God the Father, the Pantocrator", to the final prayer prayed by the priest with the paten raised above his head following communion "Have mercy on us O God our Saviour". Pleading for mercy expresses the spirit of repentance that the church continuously practices, and her confidence in the love of our good God. "God, who is rich in mercy, because of His great love with which He loved us" (Ephesians 2:4). He grants us His abundant mercy: "Let us therefore come boldly to the throne of grace, that we may obtain mercy and find grace to help in time of need" (Hebrews 4:16).

Indeed, the Divine Liturgy is a journey of repentance and obtaining mercy.

We attain "Mercy of Peace" and present the "Sacrifice of Praise."

Some may think they are righteous and call others to repentance, believing they don't need it themselves. Sometimes, this feeling is built on the assumption that sin is only adultery, theft, and murder! However, the Holy Scriptures reveal to us that "we all stumble in many things" (James 3:2). And that "if we say that we have no sin, we deceive ourselves, and the truth is not in us" (1 John 1:8). Also, "If we say that we have not sinned, we make Him a liar, and His word is not in us" (1 John 1:10).

Small and hidden sins are more dangerous than the apparent major sins. "For whoever shall keep the whole law, and yet stumble in one point, he is guilty of all" (James 2:10). Any sin, no matter how small, leads to death. "For the wages of sin is death" (Romans 6:23), such as anger, insulting others, etc. "But I say to you that whoever is angry with his brother without a cause shall be in danger of the judgment. And whoever says to his brother, 'Raca!' shall be in danger of the council. But whoever says, 'You fool!' shall be in danger of hell fire" (Matthew 5:22).

So, my friend, don't trust yourself if you consider yourself pure and honest. Before volunteering to advise people to care about the salvation of their souls and eternity, make sure you, yourself, don't need repentance. Examine your depths, lest there be a lurking sin at the door. "Do you not know that a little leaven leavens the whole lump?" (1 Corinthians 5:6).

A small sin like self-admiration, irritation, envy, etc., can lead to eternal loss, just like adultery, murder, and theft. "Let us not become conceited, provoking one another, envying one another" (Galatians 5:26). Also, other sins that we may not notice their danger, such as: "sorcery, enmity, strife, jealousy, anger, selfishness, divisions, heresies" (Galatians 5:20).

Fear and lying are counted among the sins that cause eternal destruction. "But the cowardly, unbelieving, abominable, murderers, sexually immoral, sorcerers, idolaters, and all liars shall have their part in the lake which burns with fire and brimstone, which is the second death" (Revelation 21:8).

The hardness of the heart alone is sufficient to lose a person's eternity, regardless of justifications. "For judgment is without mercy to the one who has shown no mercy. Mercy triumphs over judgment" (James 2:13).

Vanity and rejoicing in the praise of people may cost a person their precious eternal life. Condemning others, mocking people, hurting their feelings, feeling superior to others, supremacy, and using money in ways that don't glorify God and serve others are considered sins. The use of money for stumbling purposes and in extravagant actions is sinful.

Flattery, insincere and misplaced compliments, and accepting them from the other party are all hidden sins. Thus, the psalmist cries out: "Who can understand his errors? Cleanse me from secret faults" (Psalm 19:12). For they are "little foxes that spoil the vines" (Song of Solomon 2:15).

Stubbornness, clinging to one's opinion, and not seeking the advice of others are all considered sins that may jeopardize our eternal hope. Refusing to do good is also counted as a sin. "Therefore, to him who knows to do good and does not do it, to him it is sin" (James 4:17).

In the second coming, some people will perish not because they didn't believe in Christ or committed sins and didn't repent, but because they refrained from doing good deeds. "Then He will also say to those on the left hand, 'Depart from Me, you cursed, into the everlasting fire prepared for the devil and his angels: for I was hungry and you gave Me no food; I was thirsty and you gave Me no drink; I was a stranger and you did not take Me in, naked and you did not clothe Me, sick and in prison and you did not visit Me.' Then they also will answer Him, saying, 'Lord, when did we see You hungry or thirsty or a stranger or naked or sick or in prison, and did not minister to You?' Then He will answer them, saying, 'Assuredly, I say to you, inasmuch as you did not do it to one of the least of these, you did not do it to Me.' And these will go away into everlasting punishment, but the righteous into eternal life" (Matthew 25:41-46).

Sometimes, sin wears the guise of virtue. Stubbornness takes the name of defending the truth, anger appears as zeal for the sacred, pedantism masquerades as discipline, prejudice dons the mask of wisdom, and double standards cloak themselves as discerning between right and wrong. Indeed, Jesus rebuked the scribes and Pharisees not for an apparent sin but for these sins cloaked in the garment of righteousness. There is also the sin of hypocrisy "The scribes and the Pharisees sit in Moses' seat.Therefore whatever they tell you to observe, that observe and do, but do not do according to their works; for they say, and do not do."(Matthew 23:2-3)

If we search our depths, we will find that we are all sinners, and this will drive us to have compassion on other sinners (like us), and motivate us all to repent. Repentance from the Christian perspective is a continuous life-long endeavour, unto the very last breath. Everyone needs repentance because:

"They have all turned aside, they have together become corrupt; there is none who does good, no, not one." (Psalm 14:3).

"There is none righteous, no, not on" (Romans 3:10).

"for all have sinned and fall short of the glory of God" (Romans 3:23).

"For we all stumble in many things" James (3:2).

The door of repentance is open to everyone, and all sins need repentance no matter how small. Those are which the Holy Bible describes as "The little foxes that spoil the vines" (Song of Songs 2:15). The divine liturgy, along with all the church's liturgical prayers, adopt this concept; for despite the priest being considered by the church as a father, teacher, saint, leader and orchestrator, is the first called to repentance.

In the prayer of preparation that the priest prays inaudibly before setting up the altar, he prays with humility and genuine repentance of the heart saying, "O Lord, who knows the hearts of all, who is holy, and who rests in His saints; who alone is without sin and who has power to forgive sins; You O Lord, know my unworthiness and unpreparedness and my lack of meetness for this Your holy service…"

Notice, dear reader, the contrition that the priest speaks in in the presence of the Lord before commencing his holy service. Also, how he appeals to the kindness of God's loving heart, by saying that He knows the hearts and rests in His saints, and that He is alone without sin. This is as if he is saying "O Lord I want You to rest in me but I am falling short because I am a sinner, and that is not surprising, because You alone are without sin".

Deacons and priests who serve the altar know very well that it is impossible for anyone to come forward for service when they are not ready. Therefore, the liturgical service teaches me to say, "I am not worthy, or prepared and lack meetness", for regardless of how much a man undertakes the necessary preparations to serve God, he still considers himself impure. This is according to Christ's teaching, "So likewise you, when you have done all those things which you are commanded, say, 'We are unprofitable servants. We have done what was our duty to do.'" (Luke 17:10).

Thus, a person always feels unworthy, as per St Paul's saying, "For I know of nothing against myself, yet I am not justified by this; but He who judges me is the Lord." (1 Corinthians 4:4). This is to say, that even though man may not feel deficient or liable in the service in his own eyes, he cannot justify himself. Thus, what is required, is to make all necessary and appropriate preparations then stand before God in loving-fear saying "I am not prepared".

Then the priest continues his inaudible prayer saying, "and I do not have countenance to draw near and open my mouth before Your holy glory, but according to the multitude of Your tender mercies, pardon me, a sinner. And grant to me that I may find grace and mercy at this hour, and send down to me strength from on high that I may begin and make ready and accomplish Your holy service…". This deep prayer truly expresses the beautiful spirit of repentance which is accepted before God.

The stance that the priest adopts in his prayer is the same stance that Christ described in the parable of the pharisee and the tax collector "Also He spoke this parable to some who trusted in themselves that they were righteous, and despised others: "Two men went up to the temple to pray, one a Pharisee and the other a tax collector. The Pharisee stood and prayed thus with himself, 'God, I thank You that I am not like other men—extortioners, unjust, adulterers, or even as this tax collector. I fast twice a week; I give tithes of all that I possess.' And the tax collector, standing afar off, would not so much as raise his eyes to heaven, but beat his breast, saying, 'God, be merciful to me a sinner!' I tell you, this man went down to his house justified rather than the other; for everyone who exalts himself will be humbled, and he who humbles himself will be exalted." (Luke 18:9-14)

The most dangerous feeling when standing before God is the feeling of superiority, worthiness, entitlement, and self-admiration. Therefore, the Church teaches us through the liturgy what we should say in the presence of God: " Do not let your mouth cause your flesh to sin, nor say before the messenger of God that it was an error. Why should God be angry at your excuse and destroy the work of your hands?" (Ecclesiastes 5:6). In reality, "we do not know what we should pray for as we ought" (Romans 8:26).

The priest continues, "Yes, O our Master, be with us; be a partner working with us. Bless us, for You are the forgiveness of our sins, the light of our souls, our life, our strength and our boldness." This echoes the biblical concept, " But by the grace of God I am what I am, and His grace toward me was not in vain… yet not I, but the grace of God which was with me. " (1 Corinthians 15:10). As Jesus Christ said, "for without Me you can do nothing" (John 15:5).

Also, in the inaudible prayer during the morning incense, the priest says, "receive to Yourself this incense at the hands of us sinners, as a sweet savour of incense unto the remission of our sins and with the rest of Your people…".

In the inaudible prayer of the return (after the priest returns to the altar from censing the church during Vespers, Matins, the Pauline and Acts), he prays on behalf of himself and his repentant people before God with deep humility and submission: "O God, who, while on the honored Cross, accepted the confession of the thief, accept to Yourself the confession of Your people and forgive them all their sins, for the sake of Your holy name, which is called upon us; according to Your mercy, O Lord, and not according to our sins".

In a beautiful and impactful chant of humility, the priest implores God during the incense offering of Vespers and Matins, and on other occasions, saying, "O God, have mercy upon us, settle mercy upon us, have compassion upon us, hear us, bless us, keep us, and help us. Take away Your anger from us, visit us with Your salvation, and forgive us our sins."

At the end of every rite (Vespers, Matins, Divine Liturgy, as well as in Baptism, Unction of the Sick , Crowning Ceremony, Liturgy of the Waters, Prostration Prayer, Burial Service, etc.), the congregation prays, "Our Father who art in the heavens…".

Then the deacon exclaims, "Bow your heads to the Lord." Bowing is distinct from prostration and knee-bending. Head-bowing signifies the humility of repentance, making the deacon's call to the people a call to collective repentance, just as the Gospel declares, "Repent, for the kingdom of heaven is at hand" (Matthew 3:2). In alignment with Jesus Christ's words, "I tell you, unless you repent, you will all likewise perish" (Luke 13:5). Likewise the teaching of our Apostle Peter to those who believed on the day of Pentecost, "Repent, and let every one of you be baptized in the name of Jesus Christ for the remission of sins" (Acts 2:38), and similarly, " Repent therefore and be converted, that your sins may be blotted out, so that times of refreshing may come from the presence of the Lord" (Acts 3:19). "Truly, these times of ignorance God overlooked, but now commands all men everywhere to repent " (Acts 17:30).

The people respond to the deacon's call, bowing their heads, saying, "Before you, O Lord..." Then the priest prays the absolutions, entreating on behalf of the penitent with words such as: "Now also we ask and entreat Your goodness, O Lover of Mankind, for Your servants, mu fathers and my brethren, and my weakness, those who bow their heads before Your holy glory. Dispense to us Your mercy and loose every bond of our sins, and if we have committed any sin against You knowingly or unknowingly, or through anguish of heart, weather in deed or in word or from faint-heartedness, O master who knows the weakness of men as the Godd One and Lover of Mankind, O God, grant us the forgiveness of our sins...".

This prayer is a profound supplication filled with the spirit of repentance, reminiscent of the prayers of repentant saints found in the Bible, such as the prayer of the Prophet Daniel: "we have sinned and committed iniquity, we have done wickedly and rebelled, even by departing from Your precepts and Your judgments. Neither have we heeded Your servants the prophets, who spoke in Your name to our kings and our princes, to our fathers and all the people of the land. O Lord, righteousness belongs to You, but to us shame of face, as it is this day—to the men of Judah, to the inhabitants of Jerusalem and all Israel, those near and those far off in all the countries to which You have driven them, because of the unfaithfulness which they have committed against You. "O Lord, to us belongs shame of face, to our kings, our princes, and our fathers, because we have sinned against You. To the Lord our God belong mercy and forgiveness, though we have rebelled against Him...we have sinned against Him. "O Lord, according to all Your righteousness, I pray, let Your anger and Your fury be turned away from Your city Jerusalem, Your holy mountain; because for our sins, and for the iniquities of our fathers, Jerusalem and Your people are a reproach to all those around us. Now therefore, our God, hear the prayer of Your servant, and his supplications, and for the Lord's sake cause Your face to shine on Your sanctuary, which is desolate. O my God, incline Your ear and hear; open Your eyes and see our desolations, and the city which is called by Your name; for we do not present our supplications before You because of our righteous deeds, but because of Your great mercies. O Lord, hear! O Lord, forgive! O Lord, listen and act! Do not delay for Your own sake, my God, for Your city and Your people are called by Your name." (Daniel 9:5-19).

And like the prayer of Solomon the Wise on the day he inaugurated the temple, saying: "When Your people Israel are defeated before an enemy because they have sinned against You, and when they turn back to You and confess Your name, and pray and make supplication to You in this temple, then hear in heaven, and forgive the sin of Your people Israel, and bring them back to the land which You gave to their fathers. "When the heavens are shut up and there is no rain because they have sinned against You, when they pray toward this place and confess Your name, and turn from their sin because You afflict them, then hear in heaven, and forgive the sin of Your servants, Your people Israel, that You may teach them the good way in which they should walk; and send rain on Your land which You have given to Your people as an inheritance. " (1 Kings 8:33-36).

Spiritual life and our relationship with God can only be restored through repeated repentance.

The washing of hands and its connection to repentance:

The priest washes his hands before offering of the lamb and again before the prayer of reconciliation. The intended meaning of this washing is that of the heart, not the hands. Therefore, while washing his hands, the priests prays with the psalm saying, "Purge me with hyssop, and I shall be clean; wash me, and I shall be whiter than snow." It is therefore evident that the washing signifies repentance more than just cleansing the hands. "Hyssop" was a plant used in bathing (comparable to a loofah). However, this meaning of hyssop is not what is intended in the Psalm. The purifying hyssop of God refers to the Blood of Jesus Christ that purifies from every sin, as apparent in the prophecy concerning the offering of the two birds, where one is sacrificed (symbolizing Christ's sacrifice) and the other is set free (symbolizing Christ's resurrection). "As for the living bird, he shall take it, the cedar wood and the scarlet and the hyssop, and dip them and the living bird in the blood of the bird that was killed over the running water" (Leviticus 14:6). "Cedarwood" symbolizes the cross, "scarlet" represents the color of Christ's blood, "hyssop" indicates the purifying effect of this precious blood, "running water" symbolises the connection between the blood of Christ and the holy Baptism. "And he shall cleanse the house with the blood of the bird and the running water and the living bird, with the cedar wood, the hyssop, and the scarlet." (Leviticus 14:52) "The blood of Jesus His Son cleanses us from all sin." (1 John 1:7)

The priest concludes the washing of hands by praying: "I will wash my hands in innocence, and go round about Your altar, O Lord". We need this innocence achieved not by the washing of hands but through the Eucharistic sacrifice. The priest may say the following prayer instead: "Hide your face from my sins, and blot out all my iniquities. Create in me a clean heart, O God, and renew a steadfast spirit within me." This is also the famous Psalm of repentance prayed by the Prophet David after his fall and repentance, which the Church has continued to sing throughout the generations, expressing the spirit of continuous and ongoing repentance.

Pope Athanasius the Apostolic says: "We must prepare to approach the heavenly oblation, and touch the heavenly food. So let us wash our hands, purify our bodies, and keep our minds from any evil. Washing moves the soul to seek purity from the Holy Spirit residing in the soul and body since baptism."

Memorials of the oblation and repentance:

While wiping the oblation bread with water, the priest prays secretly for the people, the sick, the reposed, the travelers, and the distressed. He concludes these profound spiritual prayers with a personal prayer, saying: "Remember, O Lord, my weakness, even I the poor, and forgive me my many sins." He never ceases to recall his weakness, lowliness, and numerous sins, always seeking forgiveness from the abundant mercies of the Lord. He represents the great Prophet Moses when he said, "If now I have found grace in Your sight, O Lord, let my Lord, I pray, go among us, even though we are a stiff-necked people; and pardon our iniquity and our sin, and take us as Your inheritance." (Exodus 34:9) Similarly, Solomon the Wise prayed, saying: "hear from heaven Your dwelling place, and forgive, and give to everyone according to all his ways, whose heart You know (for You alone know the hearts of the sons of men)" (2 Chronicles 6:30)

In the inaudible prayer of the Incense for the Praxis during the reading of the Praxis (a chapter from Acts), he says "purify us from all stench of sin and make us worthy to serve in holiness and righteousness before Your goodness, O Lover of Mankind, all the days of our life". The word stench connotes sin with death, akin to what was said about Lazarus the dead, "by this time there is a stench, for he has been dead four days" (John 11:39), or as the psalm expresses the state of the sinner, "My wounds are foul and festering because of my foolishness" (Psalm 38:5).

In the hymn said before the Praxis (now only said during the Great Lent), we pray saying, "Wherein God takes away, the sins of the people, through the burnt offerings, and the aroma of incense". We do not cease to ask God to lift away our sins, as for the burnt offerings, they are the multi-faceted and effective sacrifice of the Lord Christ. Therefore, when He came into the world, He said: "Sacrifice and offering You did not desire, but a body You have prepared for Me." (Hebrews 10:5).

The true aroma of incense is the scent of Christ in us, "Now thanks be to God who always leads us in triumph in Christ, and through us diffuses the fragrance of His knowledge in every place. For we are to God the fragrance of Christ among those who are being saved and among those who are perishing." (2 Corinthians 2:14-15). For it is the scent of the sacred sacrifice of Christ that dispels the stench of sin. He has "given Himself for us, an offering and a sacrifice to God for a sweet-smelling aroma" (Ephesians 5:2).

Repentance in the Sacrament of the Gospel:

During the reading of the Gospel in the Divine Liturgy, the priest stands holding the censer, censing toward the analogion/mangaleya, honoring the Holy Gospel and expressing the special presence of the Lord Christ.

While the priest incenses, he secretly prays a long and beautiful prayer called the Prayer of the Gospel praying for the sick, travelers, captives, waters, seeds, plants, salvation of people, safety of animals, salvation of the world, the president, captives, those who have fallen asleep, those who offer gifts, the distressed, and the catechumens

In this deep prayer, we express beautiful feelings of repentance. At the beginning of this litany, the priest says: "O You, Who are long-suffering, abundant in mercy and true… receive our petitions, repentance and confession upon Your holy, undefiled altar in heaven" We fervently implore Christ our God to accept our repentance and confessions, for repentance is the breath we take in every moment of our life and our spiritual struggle. This is because our good teacher our Lord Jesus alerted us to the necessity of repentance when He said with his pure mouth, "but unless you repent you will all likewise perish" (Luke 13:3).

Repentance and the Sacrament of the Veil:

Before the priest enters the sanctuary after the Gospel reading, he stands in front of the icon holder and prays the Prayer of the Veil. This is also a deep prayer filled with the spirit of humility and repentance. The priest prays before entering the sanctuary, expressing that he cannot approach God and His holiness without repentance and stands humbly before the door of His mercy, seeking permission to enter, "But as for me, I will come into Your house in the multitude of Your mercy; In fear of You I will worship toward Your holy temple" (Psalm 5:7). And like when the Lord said to Moses the archprophet, "Do not draw near this place. Take your sandals off your feet, for the place where you stand is holy ground" (Exodus 3:5).

The expressions of repentance in this prayer include, "We ask You, O our Master, turn us not back when we put our hands on this awesome and bloodless sacrifice. For we put no trust in our righteousness, but in Your mercy. We ask and entreat Your goodness, O Lover of Mankind, that this mystery which You have administered to us for our salvation may not be unto condemnation to us or to any of Your people, but unto the wiping out of our sins and the forgiveness of our negligence…"

We do not hope for the remedy to become an illness, for the blessed Apostle Paul warned us to be cautious when approaching the Holy Mysteries, saying: "Therefore whoever eats this bread or drinks this cup of the Lord in an unworthy manner will be guilty of the body and blood of the Lord" (1 Corinthians 11:27). So, repentance is crucial for anyone approaching the life-giving Mysteries.

In another prayer of the Veil, the priest says: "Grant me at this hour a wise and understanding heart. Forgive my sins. Grant me the purity of soul, body, and spirit, that I may deserve to approach Your holy altar."

Forgiveness, wisdom, purity, and worthiness for service are sacred gifts from God for those who humble themselves before Him. It does not depend on personal righteousness but on the mercy of our good God:

"O Lord God of Israel, You are righteous, for we are left as a remnant, as it is this day. Here we are before You, in our guilt, though no one can stand before You because of this!" (Ezra 9:15).

"Not unto us, O Lord, not unto us, but to Your name give glory, because of Your mercy, because of Your truth" (Psalm 115:1).

"And now we cannot open our mouths; we, your servants who worship you, bear shame and reproach." (Prayer of Azariah 1:10).

Repentance in the great litany of peace and the litany of assemblies

In the great litany of peace

In the Great Peace Intercessions, where we pray for the peace of the Church, the state, neighbors, and everyone. We also present supplications for repentance, "let not the death of sins have dominion over us, we Your servants nor over all Your people". For sin is death, "for the wages of sin is death, but the gift of God is eternal life in Christ Jesus our Lord." (Romans 6:23). We pray that this death does not prevail over us, but that we attain eternal life as a good gift from God, the Lover of Mankind.

In the litany of assemblies

In the litany of assemblies we learn the secret to purity, which is in the prayer that says "houses of prayer, houses of purity, houses of blessing". Therefore, if you want your house to be filled with blessings, it must be a pure house. This purity comes only through prayer filled with humility, repentance, and a sense of God's presence in our lives and in our homes and places of presence.

In the same litany we pray for the complete uprooting of idol worship from the world, that is, sin in all its forms, not just bowing to idols. There are other idols in our lives, such as the love of money, dignity, ego, and the various lusts, as well as, other evil habits and negativities that have attached themselves to our personalities, which we do not want to act upon.

The Church prays for all these things to be completely uprooted by God from us, to crush Satan quickly under our feet, nullify doubts and heresies that attract people to perdition. The Church prays for the defeat of the enemies of the Church, namely, the demons who are tirelessly seeking to bring believers into corruption and destruction. "trample and humiliate them... abolish... strip their vanity, show their weakness speedily, bring to naught their envies, their intrigues, their madness, their wickedness, and their slanders, which they commit against us... bring them all to no avail... disperse their counsel, O God, who dispersed the counsel of Ahithophel".

There are phrases in the Holy Liturgy that express the spirit of repentance

For example, in the "Prayer of Reconciliation," we speak with our good God about the precious economy of salvation He devised for all humans because of His love and righteousness. The person who prays deeply and contemplatively can apply this economy of salvation in his own life and relationship with Jesus Christ saying "O God the great the eternal wo created me pure, holy, and innocent as a pure and unblemished child… but death crawled its way into my nature through the envy of the devil… and corruption and stench encroached me … death, evil and all reprehensible things overpowered me… but You O Good One did not leave me, but defeated this death by Your appearance in my life… when I return to you in repentance and confession, You bring me back to life and give me a peace that fills my entire being… so I praise with the angles saying "Glory to God in the highest, peace on earth and good will towards men".. Truly glory to You O my God in Your heavens and in every spirit that lives there… and may Your peace which is beyond comprehension reign on my earth (my body), and may I feel Your good will at my return O you the loving Father".

Also in the spirit of contrition and humility, these which God cannot reject because "He is near to those who have a broken heart, and saves such as have a contrite spirit." (Psalm 34:18_

True prayer is offered in the spirit of humility. "The sacrifices of God are a broken spirit, a broken and a contrite heart, these, O God, You will not despise" (Psalm 51:17). He also "heals the brokenhearted and binds up their wounds." (Psalm 147:3). By this beautiful spirit, the priest prays, saying, "According to Your good will, O God, fill our hearts with your peace. Cleanse us from all blemish, all guile, all hypocrisy, all craftiness, and the remembrance of vice bearing death". We feel the presence of all these pitfalls in our lives, and desire God the true physician and healer to heal the wounds of our souls, cleanse us from these imperfections, and prevent us from remembering our sins, causing us to fall back into them.

These supplications are requested from You, our righteous Father, understanding the depth of Your love and Your ability to heal us, so that the Holy Kiss may be free from all blemish, and with it, we reconcile with one another. This is so that we may be worthy of partaking of Your immortal and heavenly gifts without being cast into condemnation. Instead, may they become a source of life, salvation, and forgiveness of sins.

In the prayer of Agios (Holy):

And with the same sentiments, we pray in the prayer of Agios: "You are truly holy, O Lord, my God, and all that You do is holy, beneficial, befitting, and gracious. Therefore, You exalted me and placed me in the paradise of joy. I felt a joy that cannot be expressed, and my life was peaceful surpassing all understanding. However, I disobeyed Your commandment by the deceit of Satan, and I fell from all these privileges, and I was exiled from the life of joy. You, O Holy Lord, did not abandon me to the end but, as a good Shepherd, You have sought after that which had gone astray. As a true father, You have travailed with me, I who had fallen. You constantly bound me through Your holy saints, confessors, church educators, preachers, and interpreters of Your holy scriptures, and all who served You, to bring me back to Your divine embrace. You did not stop there but gave of Yourself and revealed to me Your love and person while I was still sitting in the darkness and shadows of death. I did not seek You, but You sought me out, for You are a compassionate Father who does not desire the death of the sinner but wishes him to return and live. You showed mercy to my weakness, taught me the ways of salvation, and granted me the grace of divine sonship through the holy baptism. That birth from above by water and the Spirit opened for me the door of repentance to reclaim the garments of sonship every time I fell. You placed the ring of the Holy Spirit on my finger and fed me with the fattened calf on Your pure altar to bring me back to You on Your shoulders, rejoicing. So, I cry out with the prophet Micah," do not rejoice over me, my enemy; when I fall, I will arise; when I sit in darkness, the Lord will be a light to me." (Micah 7:8). And once again, I join Your people, gathering around You, enjoying Your fatherhood and care. Moreover, You consider me a pure saint by Your Holy Spirit, despite my wretched transgressions and offenses. But You are the loving God who loved His own who are in the world, "having loved His own who were in the world, He loved them to the end" (John 13:1). And You surrendered Yourself as a ransom for us unto death, which had dominion over us, "the Son of God, who loved me and gave Himself for me" (Galatians 2:20), "and walk in love, as Christ also has loved us and given Himself for us, an offering and a sacrifice to God for a sweet-smelling aroma." (Ephesians 5:2).

Truly, my good God, You loved me to such an extent while I still stumbled in my sins. Do not measure Your divine love according to my deserving; forgive me.

The whole liturgy is, in essence, a journey back to God, and this is the true meaning of repentance. Therefore, the Anaphora begins with the phrase "The Lord be with you all," then "Lift up your hearts," (They are with the Lord).

My Lord Jesus, my good God. After I left you because of my many sins, and I could not see You because of the iniquities of my heart, I see you now coming to find me with your righteousness and be with me. I thank you that You have come back for me. Let me lift up my heart to you, and may it always be with you. May what I began in the liturgy never end, but may you be with me in my entrances and exits so that I may hear your divine voice saying:

"Now, my son, may the Lord be with you; and may you prosper" (1 Chronicles 22:11).

"The Lord is with you while you are with Him. If you seek Him, He will be found by you" (2 Chronicles 15:2).

"The Lord shall preserve you from all evil; He shall preserve your soul. The Lord shall preserve your going out and your coming in from this time forth, and even forevermore. " (Psalm 121:7-8).

All the prayers of the liturgy and every liturgical prayer calls us ot repentance. We can meditate on every word we say with a spirit of repentance. We can pray the words of the liturgy secretly and personally while the priest prays them aloud with the congregation. You can get lost in the meaning of the words, and get sated with the spirit of repentance and return to the warm and comforting embrace of Christ.

Just as the Anaphora begins with a request for mercy and the presence of God in our lives, it concludes with a plea for sanctification and purification: "Purify us, O Lord, from our hidden and manifest sins. Any thought that does not please Your righteousness, O God, lover of mankind, let it be far from us. Purify our souls, bodies, spirits, hearts, eyes, thoughts, and intentions. So that with a pure heart, an enlightened soul, an unashamed face, a faith unfeigned, complete love, and steadfast hope, we may boldly, without fear, pray to You, O God, who is in the heavens."

My Lord Jesus, let me approach to partake, even though I know I am not worthy, but I am in need! Do not deprive me of drawing near to Your holy altar, to nourish me with the food of eternal life. My Lord Jesus, I fear partaking, lest I be condemned! And I fear not partaking, lest I die! Therefore, let me dare to draw near to Your holy altar and partake by Your grace. "A person eats and drinks unworthily when he partakes thinking himself "worthy" by his own holiness, not by the holiness of Christ."

CHAPTER 14

Incense

Our church uses incense during prayer in the Divine Liturgy, in almost all the sacred sacraments, in prayers for the departed, and in the Liturgy of the Water and Prostration Prayer. There is a special incense prayer in the evening (offering of evening incense) and another in the morning (offering of morning incense).

Incense is used daily in the ecclesiastical life throughout the year, except on Monday, Tuesday and Wednesday of Holy Week.

The history of using incense in sacred worship:

In the book of Genesis, we read that Noah built an altar to the Lord, "and offered burnt offerings on the altar. And the Lord smelled a soothing aroma" (Genesis 8:20-21). The phrase "the Lord smelled a soothing aroma" is perhaps the first reference to incense in human history, where the presentation of the sacrifice emitted a fragrant odour from the fat of the offering and the smoke of its burning, and the Lord accepted it as soothing incense.

Pagan peoples also used incense in their deviant worship, and the people of God sometimes deviated to participate with the pagans in the censing of their false gods, which angered God and led to messages of reproach and warning.

""Moreover," says the Lord, "I will cause to cease in Moab the one who offers sacrifices in the high places and burns incense to his gods." (Jeremiah 48:35).

"I will utter My judgments against them concerning all their wickedness, because they have forsaken Me, burned incense to other gods, and worshiped the works of their own hands." (Jeremiah 1:16).

"Your iniquities and the iniquities of your fathers together," says the Lord, "Who have burned incense on the mountains" (Isaiah 65:7).

"As they called them, so they went from them; they sacrificed to the Baals, and burned incense to carved images." (Hosea 11:2).

It is noteworthy here that God did not object to incense, but He objected to censing for strange gods. Incense in that context, like other means of worship such as sacrifices, prayers, fasting, feasts, etc., was used by pagan peoples in a deviant manner for the worship of creatures rather than the Creator.

This does not mean that incense is a pagan practice that infiltrated into Christian worship, just as we cannot say that prayers are a pagan practice because the pagans used to pray to their gods. Similarly, the pagans also fasted, offered sacrifices, built temples resembling our churches, but this does not mean that these practices have a pagan origin.

So, there is sacred incense presented to our living God, and there is another impure incense presented to false pagan gods.

What distinguishes divine incense in the Old Testament from pagan incense?

First: It is offered in the name of the Lord.

Second: It is offered in Jerusalem in the temple and not outside it (in the Old Testament).

God organized the use of incense in sacred worship inside the tent of meeting during the days of the Prophet Moses, and the same system continued in the temple built by Solomon the Wise until the days of the incarnation of the Son of God. We catch a glimpse of this in the story of the appearance of the angel Gabriel to the priest Zechariah, announcing the birth of John the Baptist: " So it was, that while he was serving as priest before God in the order of his division, according to the custom of the priesthood, his lot fell to burn incense when he went into the temple of the Lord... Then an angel of the Lord appeared to him, standing on the right side of the altar of incense." (Luke 1:8-11).

The spiritual meanings of incense in the Church:

Incense has beautiful meanings in our spiritual life and our relationship with God:

(1) The Presence of Christ in the Church:

Incense symbolizes the presence of the Lord Jesus in the Church, " While the king is at his table, My spikenard sends forth its fragrance" (Song of Solomon 1:12). The Church, the bride of Christ, rejoices in this presence, praises, and glorifies the fragrant aroma of Christ: "the fragrance of your good ointments" (Song of Solomon 3:1), " His cheeks are like a bed of spices, banks of scented herbs. His lips are lilies, dripping liquid myrrh." (Song of Solomon 5:13).

In the prayer of the incense evening, the priest prays, saying, "O Christ our God, the great, awesome, and true, the only-begotten Son and Logos of God the Father, ointment poured forth is Your holy name, and in every place incense is offered to Your holy name, and a pure sacrifice." When the smoke of incense rises in the altar and the church, our hearts and minds rise to joyfully witness and realize the presence of the Lord Jesus in the Church, " The temple was filled with smoke from the glory of God and from His power, and no one was able to enter the temple " (Revelation 15:8).

(2) God is Invisible:

The thick cloud of incense indicates that God is veiled, invisible, unsearchable, and unknowable. So, when the cloud of incense rises in the church, it alerts our minds to the presence of the invisible God among us because the smoke of incense obscures the vision, " Truly You are God, who hide Yourself, O God of Israel, the Savior!" (Isaiah 45:15). Therefore, most appearances of God in the Old

Covenant were through smoke and clouds:

In the vision that Abraham saw, God appeared in the form of " there appeared a smoking oven and a burning torch that passed between those pieces." (Genesis 15:17).

In the vision of Isaiah, " and the house was filled with smoke" (Isaiah 6:4) due to the presence of God.

When God descended on Mount Sinai to speak to Moses, " Now Mount Sinai was completely in smoke, because the Lord descended upon it in fire. Its smoke ascended like the smoke of a furnace" (Exodus 19:18). "So the people stood afar off, but Moses drew near the thick darkness where God was." (Exodus 20:21).

In the hymn of praise to David, when the Lord spoke to David on the day the Lord delivered him from the hand of all his enemies and from the hand of Saul, he said: " Smoke went up from His nostrils, and devouring fire from His mouth; coals were kindled by it. He bowed the heavens also, and came down with darkness under His feet." (2 Samuel 22:9-10).

Moreover, God used to descend upon the tabernacle in the form of a cloud. "Then the cloud covered the tabernacle of meeting, and the glory of the Lord filled the tabernacle. And Moses was not able to enter the tabernacle of meeting, because the cloud rested above it, and the glory of the Lord filled the tabernacle." (Exodus 40:34-35).

This was also expressed by the prophet Isaiah: "Behold, the Lord rides on a swift cloud" (Isaiah 19:1). Similarly, the prophet Ezekiel saw in a vision " a great cloud with raging fire engulfing itself; and brightness was all around it" (Ezekiel 1:4).

During the dedication of Solomon's temple, it is written: " And it came to pass, when the priests came out of the holy place, that the cloud filled the house of the Lord, so that the priests could not continue ministering because of the cloud; for the glory of the Lord filled the house of the Lord." (1 Kings 8:10-11). Solomon then praised, saying, " The Lord said He would dwell in the dark cloud" (1 Kings 8:12). "Clouds and darkness surround Him; Righteousness and justice are the foundation of His throne" (Psalm 97:2).

When we see the altar filled with incense, we realize that God is there, incomprehensible, uncontainable, and unsearchable. Everything we know and will know about God is just a drop in an endless ocean. God is truly unfathomable.

(3) Believers' Journey:

Incense symbolizes the journey of believers, for God "through us diffuses the fragrance of His knowledge in every place. For we are to God the fragrance of Christ" (2 Corinthians 2:14-15). When incense rises in the church, it reminds us of our connection with the saints and the heavenly beings.

"Who is this coming out of the wilderness like pillars of smoke, perfumed with myrrh and frankincense, With all the merchant's fragrant powders?" (Song of Solomon 3:6)

"How much better …[is] the scent of your perfumes than all spices! And the fragrance of your garments Is like the fragrance of Lebanon." (Song of Songs 4:10-11)

The Church, along with its believers, becomes a great cloud of fragrant aroma, "a cloud of witnesses" (Hebrews 12:1)

Therefore, it is said about the Church (the new Zion), "then the Lord will create above every dwelling place of Mount Zion, and above her assemblies, a cloud and smoke by day and the shining of a flaming fire by night. For over all the glory there will be a covering." (Isaiah 4:5).

(4) Incense and the prayers of the saints:

The book of Revelations reveals to us the connection between incense and the prayers of the saints: "Then another angel, having a golden censer, came and stood at the altar. He was given much incense, that he should offer it with the prayers of all the saints upon the golden altar which was before the throne. And the smoke of the incense, with the prayers of the saints, ascended before God from the angel's hand. Then the angel took the censer, filled it with fire from the altar, and threw it to the earth. And there were noises, thunderings, lightnings, and an earthquake." (Revelations 8:3-5).

This is why, whenever incense is raised in the Church, the congregation chants doxologies and praises to the saints like verses of cymbals, hymn of intercessions, etc. This is so we share with them in the prayer, praise and rejoicing of our Lord Christ. When the aroma of the incense diffuses throughout the Church, one should consult their conscience and ask themselves: Do I emit a fragrant aroma amongst people, or is it polluted with the stench of sin? Is my fragrance like that of my saintly forefathers, the myrrh and frankincense-fragranced cloud of witnesses… or do I carry the smell of sin and the putrid body? God have mercy on me.

(5) Fellowship of the Heavenly:

The incense also symbolises the lives of the saints. The saints sublimate and ascend with their hearts, senses and prayers to Heaven like the ascending rings of incense. This is in contrary to the earthly, who are tethered to the earth and material things, and are dragged down by their desires, trespasses and transgressions. Thus, incense reminds us of our connection to the saints and the Heavenly.

During the chanting of the hymn of "Agios (Holy)", the priest takes the censer and offers incense during the hymn, before the litany of the Gospel. This signifies our participation with the heavenly beings who sing "Holy" and offer incense before the divine throne. "We ask You, O our Master, receive our prayers to Yourself. Let our prayers be set before You as incense…We ask you O lover of mankind to smell our supplications which we offer to You with incense as a pleasing sacrifice" (evening incense).

Lord Jesus, allow me to be heavenly, and may my mind and heart ascend like the incense before you. May my hope and my joy be where You abide.

(6) The Necessity of Pain:

Incense represents the necessity of pain in our spiritual life. For the fragrance of incense is only emitted when place on the fiery coals in the censor. Likewise, the sanctity of saints is only revealed when they are placed in the furnace of temptations. Temptation revealed that the substance of our father Abraham is one of obedience and faith, and highlighted the righteousness of Job. Likewise, persecution called attention to our fathers the martyrs and confessors, and proved to us the honesty of the apostles in preaching the Gospel. As for us, the believers, it is paramount to acknowledge that "We must through many tribulations enter the kingdom of God" (Acts 14:22). Thus, pain becomes a desire and a gift.

"So they departed from the presence of the council, rejoicing that they were counted worthy to suffer shame for His name." (Acts 5:41)

" For to you it has been granted on behalf of Christ, not only to believe in Him, but also to suffer for His sake" (Philippians 1:29).

"I have made myself a church for Christ, and I have arranged within it incense and fragrance with the toil of my body" (St. Ephrem the Syrian).

This is what our teacher, the Apostle Peter, expressed: "In this you greatly rejoice, though now for a little while, if need be, you have been [a]grieved by various trials, that the genuineness of your faith, being much more precious than gold that perishes, though it is tested by fire, may be found to praise, honor, and glory at the revelation of Jesus Christ" (1 Peter 1:6-7).

When I smell the fragrance of incense in the church, I realize that I must embrace the pains of Christ in my body, to be like the grain of incense, whose sweet aroma spreads to all people when it melts in the fire and ascends, and its fragrance rises to the heavens.

Perhaps this is what our teacher, the Apostle Paul, expressed in his letter to the Colossians: "I now rejoice in my sufferings for you, and fill up in my flesh what is lacking in the afflictions of Christ, for the sake of His body, which is the church" (Colossians 1:24).

Every pain we endure for the sake of Christ is counted as an offering: "Receive them upon Your holy, rational altar in heaven, as a sweet savor of incense before Your greatness in the heavens" (Litany of Oblations). Our service and the holy toil are also counted as a chosen incense: "that I may begin and make ready and accomplish Your holy service after Your pleasure, according to the assent of Your will, for a sweet savor of incense" (Prayer of the Preparation).

(7) The Passion of Christ:

The incense also represents the salvific pains of the Lord Christ: "He who offered Himself as an acceptable sacrifice on the cross for the salvation of our kind, and His righteous Father smelled Him in the evening on Golgotha." The heavenly Father and the whole world smelled the fragrance of salvation when our righteous Savior passed through the fires of the cross. Therefore, the priest puts incense in the censer during the liturgy, saying, "Was Incarnate and became man, and taught us the ways of salvation".

In the original rite, the priest places this incense using the mystir (spoon). The movement of the mystir from above the throne on the right hand-side of the chalice, to the incense box, symbolizes the incarnation of the Son of God and His descent to us on Earth.

The placement of incense in the censer symbolizes redemption through the cross, which bestowed the fragrance of salvation on the whole world, which diffused throughout the world. The priest then wipes the mystir with an altar cloth, signifying that the Lord Christ has shaken off the traces of suffering and death from His resurrected glorified body. The return of the mystir to its place beside the chalice indicates the ascent of the Lord Christ after the resurrection and His sitting at the right hand of His righteous Father.

The use of the mystir alongside the incense raises our minds to the vision seen by the Prophet Isaiah: "Then one of the seraphim flew to me, having in his hand a live coal which he had taken with the tongs from the altar. And he touched my mouth with it, and said: "Behold, this has touched your lips; your iniquity is taken away, and your sin purged."" (Isaiah 6:6-7).

Therefore, the bishop prays when consecrating the mystir saying, "O God who has made His servant Isaiah the prophet worthy of beholding the seraphim and the tongs in his hand which he picked the glowing cal from the altar and touched his mouth. Now O God the Father, the Pantocrator, extend Your hand on these spoons (mystirs) with which they will dispense the precious blood of your only begotten Son our Lord, God, and Saviour Jesus Christ. Bless them, consecrate them, and grant them the power and glory of the seraphim's togs held in his right hand. For yours is the power…."

In the litany of assemblies, when the priest prays the phrase "Houses of prayer. Houses of purity. Houses of blessing," he offers incense above the altar in the form of the cross. "For incense is the life of the Son, incorruptible, whose fragrance became sweet, offered on the altar to God the Father. The altar is the heart of the congregation, and around it stand the houses of the believers, and for this reason, the priest raises the life of the only Son, a pure and sweet fragrance to God the Father in the form of the cross, and he mentions the houses of the believers in the East, West, North, and South."

(8) Purification of the senses

The Church, during prayer, aims to engage all human senses so that one can focus on prayer and sweet conversation with our righteous Savior. The ear is filled with praises, hymns, holy readings, and preaching. The eye is satisfied with the sight of icons, curtains, the altar, and everything upon it, as well as the beauty of the God-fearing believers. The nose smells the sweet fragrance of incense, and the mind of the person is connected to the atmosphere of prayer and worship, easily entering the realm of the spiritual.

The beauty of the Church and the fragrance of incense instil reverence in the soul, lifting us to the level of prayer just upon entering the sacred church. "Ointment and perfume delight the heart" (Proverbs 27:9).

Dear Lord Jesus, let me hone in my senses on You above all else. Sanctify my eyes, and likewise my ears and nose. May I see only You, hear only Your words, and smell only Your holy and sweet fragrance.

(9) The spirit of prayer:

Incense also explains and expresses the spirit of prayer. Just as the rings of incense rise to the heavens, so do our prayers rise before the Holy God. "Let my prayer be set before You as incense" (Psalm 141:2). "I will offer to You the sacrifice of thanksgiving, and will call upon the name of the Lord" (Psalm 116:17). In the sacrifice of praise, man offers his best effort, time, and love, presenting them in joy and surrender beneath the feet of Christ, like the incense thrown on the coals, such that the fragrant smells rise to fill the vast universe with the sweet fragrance of Christ.

(10) Incense and Purification

Incense also symbolizes purification from sins. When the Israelites complained against Moses and Aaron, the anger of God was kindled, and a deadly plague struck them. "On the next day all the congregation of the children of Israel complained against Moses and Aaron, saying, "You have killed the people of the Lord." Now it happened, when the congregation had gathered against Moses and Aaron, that they turned toward the tabernacle of meeting; and suddenly the cloud covered it, and the glory of the Lord appeared. Then Moses and Aaron came before the tabernacle of meeting. And the Lord spoke to Moses, saying, "Get away from among this congregation, that I may consume them in a moment." And they fell on their faces. So Moses said to Aaron, "Take a censer and put fire in it from the altar, put incense on it, and take it quickly to the congregation and make atonement for them; for wrath has gone out from the Lord. The plague has begun." Then Aaron took it as Moses commanded, and ran into the midst of the assembly; and already the plague had begun among the people. So he put in the incense and made atonement for the people. And he stood between the dead and the living; so the plague was stopped. Now those who died in the plague were fourteen thousand seven hundred, besides those who died in the Korah incident. So Aaron returned to Moses at the door of the tabernacle of meeting, for the plague had stopped." (Numbers 16:41-50).

We, too, may be struck by the plague of sin, leading to eternal destruction. Therefore, we need the censer of Aaron to stop the plague. Perhaps this is the reason the priest takes the censer, fills it with incense, and goes to the assembly (the church's sanctuary). Like Aaron the priest, he offers a silent repentance, and then the priest returns to the sanctuary to pray the prayer of the people's confession (prayer of repentance). Through this prayer, we obtain forgiveness through the worthiness of Christ's blood.

Incense

Prayer of the People's Confession

These are purifying moments. The congregation stands, bows their heads, and secretly confesses their sins. The priest then returns to the sanctuary to pray the prayer of the people's confession, saying, "O God who accepted to Him, the confession of the thief on the honored cross, accept to You, the confession of Your people, forgive them their sins for the sake of Your Holy Name which is called upon us, Let it be according to Your mercy, O Lord, and not according to our sins."

The purifying action of the incense is also evident in the prayer the priest says during the Raising of Morning Incense: "Receive to Yourself this incense at the hands of us sinners, as a sweet savor of incense unto the remission of our sins and with the rest of Your people." The purifying meaning of incense explains why the priest censes his hands before touching the offering in the liturgy.

Lord Jesus, I need for my father the priest to fill his censer with the incense of Your love and salvation, and envelop me with the cloud of this incense, so that I may be purified with your precious blood. Allow me to repent in these moments so that I may benefit from the prayers of the church and its incense on my behalf. "

Lord Jesus, I need my father the priest to fill his censer with the incense of your love and sacrifice and to envelop me in the cloud of this smoke. I need to be purified from my sins by your precious blood. Let me repent in these moments, benefit from the prayers of the church, and its incense on my behalf. "Wherein God takes away the sins of the people, through the burn offering and the aroma of incense" (Hymn sung during Great Lent).

(11) Incense as an Act of Worship

In addition to the beautiful meanings we discussed regarding incense, its use in the church and its symbolism, we must not forget that it is also an act of worship and a sacred offering. Therefore, we find that God commanded the prophet Moses in the Old Covenant to make a special altar for incense.

a) The Altar of Incense in the Old Covenant

"You shall make an altar to burn incense on; you shall make it of acacia wood… And you shall put it before the veil that is before the ark of the Testimony, before the mercy seat that is over the Testimony, where I will meet with you. "Aaron shall burn on it sweet incense every morning; when he tends the lamps, he shall burn incense on it. And when Aaron lights the lamps at twilight, he shall burn incense on it, a perpetual incense before the Lord throughout your generations. 9 You shall not offer strange incense on it, or a burnt offering, or a grain offering; nor shall you pour a drink offering on it." (Exodus 30:1, 6-9).

The altar of incense is the one on the right side of which the angel Gabriel appeared to announce the birth of John the Baptist to the priest Zechariah. " So it was, that while he was serving as priest before God in the order of his division, according to the custom of the priesthood, his lot fell to burn incense when he went into the temple of the Lord. And the whole multitude of the people was praying outside at the hour of incense. Then an angel of the Lord appeared to him, standing on the right side of the altar of incense. " (Luke 1:8-11).

The term "altar of incense" indicates that incense was a sacred offering presented to God along with the blood sacrifices in the Old Testament. Some may think that this is limited to the Old Testament, but the texts of the Holy Scripture clearly show that incense offering continues and extends to the worship of the New Testament as well.

Prophecy about the Incense of the New Testament:

"For from the rising of the sun, even to its going down, My name shall be great among the Gentiles; in every place incense shall be offered to My name, and a pure offering; for My name shall be great among the nations,"Says the Lord of hosts." (Malachi 1:11). The prophet Malachi speaks about incense to the Lord among the nations and everywhere, not just in Jerusalem. Thus, he is not speaking about the Jewish ritual (which requires offering incense only in the Jerusalem temple), nor about pagan incense (as he speaks of incense offered to the Lord and not to idols). He specifically speaks about Christian incense, offered to God, not to idols, everywhere and not just in Jerusalem and among the Gentiles, not just among the Jews. Therefore, the priest prays in the evening prayer of incense, saying, "O Christ our God, the great, awesome, and true, the only begotten Son and Logos of God the Father, ointment poured fourth is Your holy name, and in every place incense is offered to Your holy name, and a pure sacrifice".

b) Frankincense as a gift from the Magi:

The Magi presented three gifts to the infant Jesus, each symbolizing one of His three incarnated attributes. "And when they had opened their treasures, they presented gifts to Him: gold, frankincense, and myrrh" (Matthew 2:11). The Fathers interpreted that gold was a symbol of His kingship, myrrh a symbol of His life-giving sufferings and death, and frankincense (incense) a sign of His priesthood and divinity. It signifies the true God manifest in the flesh, being both a king, a priest, and a saviour. When we offer incense in our prayers, we express our faith in His divinity, just as the Magi did in ancient times.

c) Composition of Incense:

The incense used in worship had precise specifications and a unique sanctity. It was not allowed for anyone to make or use it in their homes. The Lord said to Moses, " And the Lord said to Moses: "Take sweet spices, stacte and onycha and galbanum, and pure frankincense with these sweet spices; there shall be equal amounts of each. You shall make of these an incense, a compound according to the art of the perfumer, salted, pure, and holy. And you shall beat some of it very fine, and put some of it before the Testimony in the tabernacle of meeting where I will meet with you. It shall be most holy to you. But as for the incense which you shall make, you shall not make any for yourselves, according to its composition. It shall be to you holy for the Lord. Whoever makes any like it, to smell it, he shall be cut off from his people." (Exodus 30:34-38).

This precise specification reveals God's regard for the incense offering, its sanctity, and its dedication to the service of the Lord's holies. Similarly, in Christian thought, it is not permitted for individuals to use church incense in their homes. In the Coptic rite, only the priest is allowed to cense, and deacons are not permitted to do so because censing is a function of the priesthood.

Biblical Stories:

There is a story in the Old Testament that reinforces this meaning. The people of Korah, Dathan, and Abiram dared to offer incense to the Lord, and the Lord's anger burned against them. "And fire came out from the Lord and consumed the two hundred and fifty men who were offering incense" (Numbers 16:35) because they were not priests and had no right to offer incense. This punishment was "a memorial to the children of Israel that no outsider, who is not a descendant of Aaron, should come near to offer incense before the Lord, that he might not become like Korah and his companions" (Numbers 16:40).

Another Biblical story:

The following was said about King Uzziah, "when he was strong his heart was lifted up, to his destruction, for he transgressed against the Lord his God by entering the temple of the Lord to burn incense on the altar of incense. So Azariah the priest went in after him, and with him were eighty priests of the Lord—valiant men. And they withstood King Uzziah, and said to him, "It is not for you, Uzziah, to burn incense to the Lord, but for the priests, the sons of Aaron, who are consecrated to burn incense. Get out of the sanctuary, for you have trespassed! You shall have no honor from the Lord God." Then Uzziah became furious; and he had a censer in his hand to burn incense. And while he was angry with the priests, leprosy broke out on his forehead, before the priests in the house of the Lord, beside the incense altar. ... so they thrust him out of that place" *(2 Chronicles 26"16-20). Thus Uzziah suffered the consequence of overstepping and disrespecting priest-only roles.

"Now thanks be to God who always leads us in triumph in Christ, and through us diffuses the fragrance of His knowledge in every place. For we are to God the fragrance of Christ among those who are being saved and among those who are perishing." (2 Corinthians 2:14-15)

Procession of incense in the Church:

After the Thanksgiving Prayer in the rite of raising of incense in matins and vespers, the priest enters the sanctuary and places five spoonfuls of incense in the censer. While doing so he recites the appropriate prayers in the name of the Holy Trinity on the incense box. Then, he prays the prayer of raising incense for Vespers or Matins, depending on the time of prayer.

During Vespers, the priest prays secretly, "O Christ our God, the great, awesome, and true, the only-begotten Son and Logos of God the father, ointment poured forth is Your holy name, and in every place incense is offered to Your holy name, and a pure sacrifice. We ask You, O our Master, receive our prayers to Yourself. Let our prayers be set forth before You as incense, the lifting up of our hands, the evening sacrifice. For You are the true evening sacrifice, who has offered Yourself upon the honoured Cross for our sins according to the will of Your good Father, with whom You are blessed with the Holy Spirit, the Giver of Life, who is of one essence with You, now and at all times and unto the ages of all ages. Amen".

As for during Matins, the priest secretly prays, " O God who received to Yourself the offerings of the righteous Abel, the sacrifice of Noah and Abraham and the incense of Aaron and Zechariah receive to Yourself this incense at the hands of us sinners, as a sweet savour of incense unto the remission of our sins and with the rest of Your people. For blessed and full of glory is Your holy name, O Father and Son and Holy Spriit, now and at all times and unto the ages of all ages. Amen".

Then the priest goes around the altar, opposite him the deacon, praying three small litanies which are (the peace of the church, the patriarch and bishops, then assemblies). Then the priest exists the altar to cense outside it and in front of the icons and the gospel. Then he goes down to the navel of the church to bless the congregation with the incense. The procession through the navel of the church occurs during the raising of evening incense, raising of morning incense, during the chanting of the doxologies and during the Pauline and the Pauline response. However, the procession of incense during the Praxis is limited to the front part of the navel only. Then the priest goes back into the altar to pray the prayer for the confession of the people, considering the priest's rotation in the church as an opportunity for a quick confession (for those who desire). This is in addition to the opportunity for collective repentance for the entire congregation, where they confess their sins from the heart before God. Of course, this quick, secret confession or public confession does not replace the practice of the sacrament of confession in private. Many biblical references emphasize the necessity of confession before a priest:

1. People confessing to John the Baptist: "and [they] were baptized by him in the Jordan, confessing their sins" (Matthew 3:6).

2. Achan confessing before Joshua: "Now Joshua said to Achan, "My son, I beg you, give glory to the Lord God of Israel, and make confession to Him, and tell me now what you have done; do not hide it from me."" (Joshua 7:19).

3. The people confessing before Nehemiah after returning from captivity: "Then those of Israelite lineage separated themselves from all foreigners; and they stood and confessed their sins and the iniquities of their fathers." (Nehemiah 9:2).

4. Sirach's advice regarding confession: "You should not be ashamed to confess your sins" (Sirach 4:31).

5. James's exhortation: "Confess your trespasses to one another, and pray for one another, that you may be healed. The effective, fervent prayer of a righteous man avails much." (James 5:16).

6. The actions of the early apostles: "And many who had believed came confessing and telling their deeds." (Acts 19:18).

Incense

7. The authority given to the priests by Christ regarding forgiveness of sins: "If you forgive the sins of any, they are forgiven them; if you retain the sins of any, they are retained." (John 20:23). "Assuredly, I say to you, whatever you bind on earth will be bound in heaven, and whatever you loose on earth will be loosed in heaven." (Matthew 18:18).

8. Proverbs' advice: "He who covers his sins will not prosper, But whoever confesses and forsakes them will have mercy." (Proverbs 28:13).

The relationship between the sacrament of confession and the opportunity for repentance during the liturgy in the censing and other opportunities is complementary; one does not replace the other.

In every liturgy, I need to repent and confess to God, and in every liturgical prayer, I need for my father, the priest, to pray for me, along with the congregation, several times (at the end of vespers, the end of matins, before the absolution of servants, and after the fraction). I also need to hear the priest pray a personal absolution, saying, "Your servant - so-and-so – and my weakness be absolved from my own moth and from the mouth of the All Holy Trinity"

Lord Jesus, let me not miss any opportunity for repentance, and let me hear the absolution and forgiveness from the mouth of my father, the priest, with Your Holy Spirit, both personally and collectively.

Between eternity and time

We notice that the movement of the priest when he exits with the censer is always counterclockwise, and this is the direction of any procession in the church. This means that the church is above time; it is not subject to it because it has entered eternity.

In the censing procession during the Praxis, the movement is clockwise, following the movement of the sun, which also has a beautiful spiritual meaning. Despite the church being above time (opposite to the movement of the sun), it exists in time to serve across time.

The Praxis is the Acts of the apostles, whose role was to transform the material world into a spiritual world and the wicked into saints.

The church must descend into the world to lift it to eternity, and the priest descends into the world to preach and proclaim, then returns to the sanctuary to present this congregation to God.

The only time we move clockwise around the church during an incense procession is during the Procession of Judas on the Matins of Covenant Thursday, announcing that Judas has lost his eternity because of his love for money and denial of Christ. This is a warning for every soul that betrays Christ the Bridegroom.

CHAPTER 15

Saints in the Liturgy

We frequently mention the names of the saints in the Divine Liturgy in the Commemoration of the Saints, Hymn of the Intercessions, Verses of Cymbals, Doxologies, veneration following the Synaxarion, during the Absolution of the Servants, Praxis response and among many other occasions.

So, why are we attached to them and their intercessions? Why do we have relationships and interactions with them? Why do we name churches after them? And why do we preserve their holy relics, take their blessings, and celebrate their feasts?

To understand this, let's first recognize that the Bible itself commands us to love and honor the saints:

"Remember those who rule over you, who have spoken the word of God to you, whose faith follow, considering the outcome of their conduct." (Hebrews 13:7).

In the account of the Transfiguration, the Lord Jesus did not appear alone; Moses and Elijah were with Him:

"And Elijah appeared to them with Moses, and they were talking with Jesus." (Mark 9:4).

The glory of Christ does not preclude glorifying the saints with Him, and the glorification of the saints does not diminish the glory of the Lord Jesus in any way. As humans, we are called to respect every person on earth, without despising or belittling them. For each human being is worthy of dignity, believer or not,

" Honor all people. Love the brotherhood. Fear God. Honor the king." (1 Peter 2:17).

The dignity of a person increases when they are a faithful and righteous believer. A baptized Christian, anointed with the Holy Myron, united with the Body and Blood of the Lord in the sacrament of Communion, who prays and sanctifies their body, experiences a profound increase in dignity. If that is the case, how dignified are the saints who completed their lives on earth in piety. The saints are members of the body of Christ, just as we are also members. That in and of itself is a great honour… "For we are members of His body, of His flesh and of His bones." (Ephesians 5:30). In addition to this, we are a temple of the Holy Spirit:

"Do you not know that you are the temple of God and that the Spirit of God dwells in you?... For the temple of God is holy, which temple you are." (1 Corinthians 16:3-17).

The saints are present with us in the Church, and we believe in their intercessions. We honor the saints because God Himself honors them:

"for those who honor Me I will honor" (1 Samuel 2:30).

Since God honours them, it is not strange for us to honour them too. They have honoured God by fulfilling His command to "be holy," and as long as they fulfilled it, they are worthy of all honour and respect:

"You shall therefore be holy, for I am holy." (Leviticus 11:45).

"but as He who called you is holy, you also be holy in all your conduct, because it is written, "Be holy, for I am holy." (1 Peter 1:15-16).

We love them deeply and rejoice in them:

"As for the saints who are on the earth, "They are the excellent ones, in whom is all my delight"" (Psalm 16:3).

"Yes, He loves the people; All His saints are in Your hand; They sit down at Your feet; Everyone receives Your words." (Deuteronomy 33:3).

God Himself is glorified amongst His saints, for the Lord will come again at the second coming with all His saints:

"at the coming of our Lord Jesus Christ with all His saints." (1 Thessalonians 3:13).

"Behold, the Lord comes with ten thousands of His saints" (Jude 1:14).

"when He comes, in that Day, to be glorified in His saints and to be admired among all those who believe" (2 Thessalonians 1:10).

Therefore, when we venerate the saints, we glorify God through them:

"Let your light so shine before men, that they may see your good works and glorify your Father in heaven" (Matthew 5:16).

"And they glorified God in me" (Galatians 1:24).

"having your conduct honorable among the Gentiles, that when they speak against you as evildoers, they may, by your good works which they observe, glorify God in the day of visitation." (1 Peter 2:12).

Moreover, the saints will share in the judgment of the world. The Lord Jesus promised His pure disciples that they would sit on twelve thrones judging the twelve tribes of Israel:

"when the Son of Man sits on the throne of His glory, you who have followed Me will also sit on twelve thrones, judging the twelve tribes of Israel." (Matthew 19:28).

"Do you not know that the saints will judge the world? And if the world will be judged by you, are you unworthy to judge the smallest matters? Do you not know that we shall judge angels? How much more, things that pertain to this life?" (1 Corinthians 6:2-3).

God has given them a glory that surpasses description:

"And the glory which You gave Me I have given them, that they may be one just as We are one" (John 17:22).

"And he who overcomes, and keeps My works until the end, to him I will give power over the nations" (Revelation 2:26).

"He who overcomes shall be clothed in white garments, and I will not blot out his name from the Book of Life; but I will confess his name before My Father and before His angels" (Revelation 3:5).

"He who overcomes, I will make him a pillar in the temple of My God, and he shall go out no more. I will write on him the name of My God and the name of the city of My God, the New Jerusalem, which comes down out of heaven from My God. And I will write on him My new name." (Revelation 3:12).

"To him who overcomes I will grant to sit with Me on My throne, as I also overcame and sat down with My Father on His throne." (Revelation 3:21).

"He who overcomes shall inherit all things, and I will be his God and he shall be My son." (Revelation 21:7).

And the saints are those who revealed to us the will of God, as mentioned in the prophecies:

"which God has spoken by the mouth of all His holy prophets since the world began." (Acts 3:21)

"As He spoke by the mouth of His holy prophets, Who have been since the world began,The saints are those with whom we will share eternal glory" (Luke 1:70).

The saints are those with whom we'll partake of the Eternal Glory:

"giving thanks to the Father who has qualified us to be partakers of the inheritance of the saints in the light." (Colossians 1:12).

"But the saints of the Most High shall receive the kingdom, and possess the kingdom forever, even forever and ever." (Daniel 7:18).

And the Lord Christ considers them as His counterparts:

"He who receives you receives Me, and he who receives Me receives Him who sent Me." (Matthew 10:40).

"He who hears you hears Me, he who rejects you rejects Me, and he who rejects Me rejects Him who sent Me." (Luke 10:16).

The saints support our spiritual struggle; they surround us and encourage us in our spiritual strife and earthly life:

"Therefore we also, since we are surrounded by so great a cloud of witnesses, let us lay aside every weight, and the sin which so easily ensnares us, and let us run with endurance the race that is set before us" (Hebrews 12:1).

The saints, whether on Earth or in Heaven, pray for us. When the Lord Christ spoke about the resurrection from the dead, He said: "'I am the God of Abraham, the God of Isaac, and the God of Jacob'? God is not the God of the dead, but of the living." (Matthew 22:32). The Lord Christ Himself testified that they are alive, and we believe that there is "no death for your servants, but a departure."

The Bible commands us: "pray for one another" (James 5:16). Our teacher James also says: "Is anyone among you sick? Let him call for the elders of the church, and let them pray over him, anointing him with oil in the name of the Lord. And the prayer of faith will save the sick, and the Lord will raise him up. And if he has committed sins, he will be forgiven." (James 5:14-15).

The principle is clear: to pray for one another.

God hears everyone's prayers, but undoubtedly, the prayers of the saints and the righteous are more impactful:

"He will fulfill the desire of those who fear Him; He also will hear their cry" (Psalm 145:19).

"The effective, fervent prayer of a righteous man avails much" (James 5:16).

This is My Body

If God fulfills the desire of those who fear Him on earth, and hears their supplications, how much more for the saints in Heaven who have completed their struggle? How great is their intercession before God!

There are many stories in the Bible of people praying acceptable prayers for others.

Abraham, the father of the patriarchs, interceded for Sodom and Gomorrah:

"And Abraham came near and said, "Would You also destroy the righteous with the wicked? 24 Suppose there were fifty righteous within the city; would You also destroy the place and not spare it for the fifty righteous that were in it? 25 Far be it from You to do such a thing as this, to slay the righteous with the wicked, so that the righteous should be as the wicked; far be it from You! Shall not the Judge of all the earth do right?"" (Genesis 18:23-25).

"Suppose ten should be found there?" And He said, "I will not destroy it for the sake of ten."" (Genesis 18:32).

Moses the prophet prayed for the people:

"Yet now, if You will forgive their sin—but if not, I pray, blot me out of Your book which You have written" (Exodus 32:32).

The prophet Samuel prayed for his people, and the Lord answered him:

"Then Samuel cried out to the Lord for Israel, and the Lord answered him." (1 Samuel 7:9).

Job the righteous prayed for his friends: "And the Lord restored Job's losses when he prayed for his friends. Indeed the Lord gave Job twice as much as he had before." (Job 42:10). He also prayed on behalf of his sons: "So it was, when the days of feasting had run their course, that Job would send and sanctify them, and he would rise early in the morning and offer burnt offerings according to the number of them all. For Job said, "It may be that my sons have sinned and cursed God in their hearts." Thus Job did regularly." (Job 1:5).

In application of the principle of praying for others, our teacher Paul the Apostle asked people to pray for him, that God would open a door for preaching the word: "meanwhile praying also for us, that God would open to us a door for the word, to speak the mystery of Christ, for which I am also in chains" (Colossians 4:3).

The glorification of the saints is a principle found in the Bible. The beautiful thing is that the Lord Christ Himself is the first to establish doxologies (doxology means glorification), praising John the Baptist:

"He began to speak to the multitudes concerning John: "What did you go out into the wilderness to see? A reed shaken by the wind? But what did you go out to see? A man clothed in soft garments? Indeed those who are gorgeously appareled and live in luxury are in kings' courts. But what did you go out to see? A prophet? Yes, I say to you, and more than a prophet. This is he of whom it is written: 'Behold, I send My messenger before Your face, Who will prepare Your way before You.' For I say to you, among those born of women there is not a greater prophet than John the Baptist; but he who is least in the kingdom of God is greater than he.' '" (Luke 7:24-28).

The Church has taken this passage and made a doxology for John the Baptist, and in the same manner, doxologies have been made for the rest of the saints. For the saints are highly honoured.

One way the Bible honours the saints is by naming books after them: (Joshua, Ruth, Samuel, Ezra, Nehemiah, Esther, Job, Isaiah, Jeremiah, Daniel, Hosea, Joel, Amos... Matthew, Mark, Luke, John).

Also, holy things are named after the saints like (the Law of Moses, Solomon's Temple, Aaron's Rod...).

It is not strange for the Church to honour the saints by naming churches after them. They are a light, pride, and an example for us. They are present with us in the Church and at all times because the Church is the house of angels and saints.

Another reason the Church cares about mentioning the names of the saints in the Divine Liturgy is that they are our fathers who handed down to us the holy faith, "the faith which was once for all delivered to the saints." (Jude 1:3), and they preserved it pure, explained it, and handed it down to us efficiently and skilfully, making what we believe today the same as what the Church believed from the beginning.

When we mention the names of these holy champions, we remember their toil and struggle for us. This honourable commemoration is praised in the Scriptures:

"Now I praise you, brethren, that you remember me in all things and keep the traditions just as I delivered them to you." (1 Corinthians 11:2).

"For you remember, brethren, our labor and toil; for laboring night and day, that we might not be a burden to any of you, we preached to you the gospel of God." (1 Thessalonians 2:9).

Indeed, the commemoration of the holy forefathers is required of us as a holy commandment in the Scriptures:

"Remember those who rule over you, who have spoken the word of God to you, whose faith follow, considering the outcome of their conduct." (Hebrews 13:7).

Mentioning the names of the saints in the liturgy in particular, declares our alliance with them and to the faith they taught and explained. When we mention the names of the saints like Athanasius the Apostolic, Cyril the Pillar of Faith, Dioscorus, Severus of Antioch, John Chrysostom, Gregory the Theologian, and others, we declare our adherence to their faith and our journey in their footsteps.

Therefore, we also mention the fathers assembled in Nicaea, Constantinople, and Ephesus, announcing our recognition of these sacred ecumenical councils and our commitment to the faith explained in them and the doctrinal texts established in them. They are the fathers who confessed the good confession of the divinity of our Lord, making them "those who were perfected in the faith"

We also mention at the beginning of the commemoration the holy and pure Virgin Mary as the one "who truly gave birth to God the Word"

We remember our pure fathers, the patriarchs, prophets, apostles, evangelists, martyrs, confessors, and all the spirits of the righteous who were "perfected in the faith." They believed in the divinity of Christ, prophesied about it, preached it, or suffered hardships and tortures or death for confessing it. Truly, it is a precious and valuable faith.

We remember John the Baptist, the forerunner and martyr because he bore witness to the Lamb of God who carries the sins of the world when he said, "And I have seen and testified that this is the Son of God." (John 1:34). And Saint Stephen, the archdeacon and the protomartyr, for he professed the divinity of Christ before the council and at the time of his martyrdom when he said, "Look! I see the heavens opened and the Son of Man standing at the right hand of God!" (Acts 7:56).

The divine evangelist Mark, the apostle and martyr, who evangelised to us the divinity of the Son, enlightening Egypt with this holy faith. He received the crown of martyrdom for the sake of this blessed proclamation.

And Saint Severus, the Patriarch of Antioch, who supported our Coptic Church against the division and slander of the Chalcedonian council that unjustly condemned our patriarch and teacher, Saint Dioscorus.

And who does not know the merit and virtue of the great Patriarch Saint Athanasius the Apostolic in his struggle to preserve the Orthodox faith against the Arian heresy? It was said to him, "The whole world is against you," and he boldly replied: "And I am against the world"! Indeed, were it not for God's preparation of this great saint for His Church, the world would have almost become Arian.

But we also, in this regard, do not forget the struggle of Patriarch Saint Peter, the archpriest, and the seal of the martyrs who started the struggle against Arianism early. Were it not for his vigilance and conscientiousness, the faith would have been lost.

The fathers continued to pass on the torch of faith with purity, skilfulness, and fidelity from generation to generation. "St. John Chrysostom, St. Theodosius, St. Theophilus, St. Demetrius, St. Cyril, St. Basil, St. Gregory the Theologian, St. Gregory the Wonderworker, and St. Gregory The Armenian" are part of this cloud of witnesses.

Within this cloud of witnesses, our holy fathers, the monks, entered, proving with their holy lives the authenticity and soundness of Orthodox faith. The Church takes pride in them in front of the heretics whose deviation in faith was accompanied by a deviation in conduct. It has been said, "The reason for the purity of the faith of Athanasius… is his piety. This reveals the meaning of the verse: "But someone will say, "You have faith, and I have works." Show me your faith without your works, and I will show you my faith by my works." (James 2:18).

In this sacred fellowship, we find our righteous father, the St. Anthony, the righteous St. Paul, the three holy Macarii, and all their children cross-bearers. We also find St. John the Hegumen, St. Pishoy, St. Paul the Ascetic, the Roman fathers Sts. Maximus and Dometius, the forty-nine elders of Shiheet, the strong St. Moses, St. John Kame, St. Daniel, St. Isidore, St. Pachomius and St. Theodore his disciple, and St. Shenouda and St. Wissa.

It is an endless chain because the Spirit of God was with Enoch, Noah, Abraham, Isaac, Jacob, Moses, Joshua, Samuel, David, Isaiah, Jeremiah, and Daniel in the Old Testament, and in the New Testament with Paul, Peter, Andrew, Matthew, Mark, Luke, John, and Barnabas. The same Spirit has not ceased to produce great saints, men of God, till today and till the end of days.

Therefore, we conclude the commemoration of the saints by amalgamating the remainder of the saints, saying: "And all the choir of Your saints, through whose prayers and supplications, have mercy on us all, and save us for the sake of Your holy name which is called upon us."

We began the commemoration by supplicating the mystery of God to remember all of His saints, then we finish it by asking for the saints' prayers and supplications on our behalf. This is the holy fellowship of prayer, in which we pray for them, and they also pray for us.

Feeling unworthy to intercede for the saints, we pray in the Liturgy of Cyril, saying: "Not that we are worthy, O Master, to intercede for the blessedness of those who are there, but rather they are standing before the tribunal of Your Only-Begotten Son, that they may be interceding instead for our poverty and our frailty. May You be a forgiver of our iniquities for the sake of their holy supplications and for the sake of Your blessed name which is called upon us."

In the Church and around the altar in the Eucharistic sacrament, the people become a united force of prayer for the bishop, and the bishop and the congregation in the presence of Christ become a force of prayer for the saints.

It is truly a beautiful symphony that declares the fellowship of love between Heaven and Earth, as we all become one in Christ, fulfilling the holy commandment:

"pray for one another…The effective, fervent prayer of a righteous man avails much." (James 5:16). "giving thanks to the Father who has qualified us to be partakers of the inheritance of the saints in the light." (Colossians 1:12).

The Synaxarion and the Antiphonary:

The mention of the names of saints and martyrs is not limited to the Commemoration of Saints alone but is also remembered on their feast days and commemorations.

The book containing the lives of the saints is called "Synaxar/Synaxarion/Synaxarium," and this word is derived from the Greek word "Synaxarion."

The feasts of the saints include the day of their repose or martyrdom, as well as the commemoration of the relocation of their relics, the building of churches in their names, or commemorations of associated famous miracles. The Synaxarion tells the history of the saint, providing a brief historical account to acquaint us with the most important events of their lives and their virtues. This narrative distinguishes it from another book called "Antiphonary," where the same biography of the saint is recounted but in the format of praise and glorification.